Performance Contracting in Education –
An Appraisal

Performance Contracting in Education – An Appraisal

Toward a Balanced Perspective

Donald M. Levine, Editor
Teachers College, Columbia University

Educational Technology Publications
Englewood Cliffs, New Jersey 07632

Library of Congress Cataloging in Publication Data

National Conference on Performance Contracting in
    Education, Washington, D.C., 1971.
    Performance contracting in education—an appraisal.

    Sponsored by the American Educational Research
Association and the American Association of School
Administrators.
    1. Performance contracts in education—Addresses,
essays, lectures. I. Levine, Donald M., ed.
II. American Educational Research Association.
III. American Association of School Administrators.
IV. Title.
LB2806.2.N37   371.1   72-12681
ISBN 0-87778-046-3

This book is based on the final report of the
National Conference on Performance Contracting in Education, held in December, 1971, and
co-sponsored by the American Educational
Research Association and the American Association of School Administrators. The conference was funded by the United States Office of
Education's National Center for Educational
Research and Development.

Library of Congress Catalog Card Number:
72-12681

International   Standard   Book   Number:
0-87778-046-3.

First Printing: December, 1972.

Table of Contents

Performance Contracting in Education –
An Appraisal

1.

Introduction

DONALD M. LEVINE

The National Conference on Performance Contracting in Education, on which this volume is based, sought to provide a user-based and user-oriented assessment of performance contracting for education. It focused on delineating the current interest in performance contracting, the technique's demonstrated strengths and weaknesses, and its potential as an alternative approach to school system resource allocation. Six commissioned papers discussed, respectively, major problems in performance contracting, the Rand-HEW evaluation of performance contracting, measurement and evaluation difficulties, a model for comparing costs of different performance contracting programs, more comprehensive measurement of educational outputs, and employment relations under performance contracting. Discussions of these papers and of administrators' experiences emphasized the many problems of measurement and evaluation that have emerged in performance contracting.

This volume contains the six commissioned papers and also the comments and conclusions of a number of invited participants at the conference. These statements about the future of perform-

Donald M. Levine, Chairman of the National Conference on Performance Contracting in Education, is Associate Professor, Department of Educational Administration, Teachers College, Columbia University.

ance contracting, found in Chapter 8, were made several months *after* the conference. They reflect the information presented in December, 1971, as well as more recent progress reports and data.

The National Conference on Performance Contracting in Education, co-sponsored by the American Educational Research Association (AERA) and the American Association of School Administrators (AASA) under a U.S. Office of Education grant, was the result of two circumstances. The first was the great growth of performance contracting for education between the 1969-1970 school year and the 1970-1971 school year. In 1969-1970, only one nationally known performance contract had been let by a public school system; in 1970-1971, more than 150 such contracts were let. At least four reasons can be cited for the swift expansion of performance contracting.

First, it seemed to hold some answers to the persistent problem of effectiveness, especially for programs designed to alleviate the specific educational deficiencies of the disadvantaged. By linking payment directly and sensitively to results, perform-ance contracting was supposed to motivate the private sector to realize fully its presumably great potential for producing signifi-cant educational changes.

Second, performance contracting seemed to insure more rational, efficient resource allocation, for it was supposed to rely explicitly on measured outcomes. A school system that lets such a contract is supposed to be buying tangible progress and paying only for value received. Moreover, certain performance contracts tried to build in future efficiency by specifying that the contractor use only cost-effective (rather than labor-intensive) methods that the school system later could adopt for proprietary use.

Third, by involving the private sector in difficult, risky enterprises, performance contracts presumably encouraged the introduction and testing of the highly productive technologies that school systems need but have been unable to use and to integrate with their curricula. These technologies are supposed to produce long-term benefits when they are transferred from the contractor to the school system and fully incorporated during the final "transfer" or "turnkey" stage of the performance contract.

Finally, performance contracting was seen both as a genuine response to increasing community and governmental demands for palpable educational results and as a possible way to counter growing community resistance to approving ever larger appropriations. When a school system requests funds for a performance contract, in effect, it was thought to show the community in more precise ways what it can buy rather than asking it to contribute to the general, undifferentiated support of a school system whose "product" is unclear.

Though these reasons seemed to have been compelling ones for implementing performance contracting, no individual or group had yet provided a comprehensive, user-based and user-oriented assessment of performance contracting. The conference sponsors felt strongly that such an assessment should be available if school systems were to continue to let performance contracts after 1970-1971.

The second circumstance which lay behind this conference was that significant experience with and evaluations of performance contracting had begun to emerge.

The conference was organized to coincide with first publication of the results of the Rand-HEW study of performance contracting and took place shortly before publication of the results of the U.S. Office of Economic Opportunity (OEO) experiment in performance contracting. Representatives of both Rand and OEO were conference participants, so the conference was able to make use of data generated by the only two broad-scale evaluations of performance contracting currently available.

In general, the present volume, based on the conference, seeks to answer questions relating to five particular aspects of performance contracting:

1. Its Origins

Performance contracting originally was a response to specific financial, managerial, and product needs of industry and government—particularly those of the Department of Defense. To develop a functional conception of performance contracting, we must understand these roots. In addition, we must clarify the educational needs which performance contracting is supposed to meet, bring out any important differences between these needs and those of government and industry, and determine whether the technique has undergone any significant alterations intended to make it more suitable for its new application. In short, we must determine why and how *educational* performance contracting differs from earlier forms. Given its roots, what can we expect of performance contracting in education (and what must we *not* expect)? For example, can we justify treating progress on a standardized test as a "product"—like a transistor or a gunsight—that either meets or fails to meet contract specifications? Is this a legitimate objective for a school system?

2. Its Structure

What are the essential elements of a performance contracting program, and how do they interact? What alternative types of performance contracts are available to the school system? We must identify those aspects of a performance contract that can be varied with the needs of a particular case in order to insure maximum benefits and to produce a true reflection of a school system's needs. This identification, of course, will demand an understanding of the dynamics of performance contracting, of its internal logic. We must examine the strengths, flexibility, pitfalls, and comparative merits of various components and types of components. For example, what kinds of evaluation measures are available, and which ones should we use in a particular case? At what times during the life of the contract can we apply them, and can we gradually adapt them to any new output quantities that may emerge as the contract is executed? How should these measures be used to determine payment? Can they be refined during the life of the contract without undermining the entire scheme of "payment for performance" that the contract embodies?

3. Its Specific Applications

Few school systems have tried to determine what circumstances favor letting a performance contract, aside from the general need for real progress in educating their "clients." Detailed consideration must be given to preconditions such as the legal and informal relations with government at all levels, the types of learning problems to be solved, and the details of the process of school finance. We also must ask how well a performance contract suits these preconditions in contrast to the suitability of competing in-house modes such as "model teaching experiments" and other, more traditional, schemes of program development, implementation, and evaluation. We must study the intra-systemic effects of performance contracting, its specific interactions with system components such as teachers, organized labor, physical facilities, accounting practices, planning frameworks, parents, and instructional activities that are not included in the contract under consideration. For example, what kinds of problems must we expect in phasing "contracted students" back into the ordinary curriculum, especially in light of the new ways of learning and different knowledge they may have acquired? More generally, how shall we determine a performance contract's relations with the goals and structure of the school system by defining the policy, managerial, and operational responsibilities of both parties to the contract?

4. Its Results to Date

What does our experience with performance contracting for education say to the aforementioned aspects of structure and application? What unexpected problems have emerged, if any? Are they inherent difficulties, or simply those of inexperience? Is there enough reliable data to generate a set of recommendations? If so, what recommendations would be most useful to the school system? To the private contractor? Until now, the almost complete lack of relevant data has precluded answering such questions; but at this point, experience can answer questions about such topics as the relationship between contractors and school system teachers and the criteria used to select "contracted pupils" from a larger target group. School administrators now can (and should) have an awareness of and reaction to the demonstrated strengths and weaknesses of performance contracting.

5. Its Future

In light of all the preceding considerations, where can performance contracting go, and where do users want it to go? School administrators must identify weaknesses that should be alleviated, strengths that should be exploited, and the role of performance contracting in the larger context of educational planning.

* * *

In more general operational terms, answering this broad variety of questions requires achievement of four objectives:

1. To cull and analyze relevant experience in performance contracting for education.
2. To identify and respond to the salient issues, which principally relate to four areas:
   a. Measurement and Evaluation;
   b. Articulation of the contractor's programs with the school system's and with elements of the school system's environment;
   c. Application of performance contracting to various types of programs—remedial, skill-training, research oriented; and externally (federally) funded programs, as well as those that cut across grade and subject lines; and
   d. Specifications of what constitutes a "good" performance contract.
3. To promote the practitioner's awareness and understanding of the issues that currently concern both researchers and administrators.
4. To identify the major features of a performance contract and the criteria used to select it, as well as to show how the contract and these criteria can best articulate school system objectives.

In response to these goals and objectives, the present volume emphasizes:

- delineating the dimensions of current interest in performance contracting, the reasons for it, and the particular school system needs to which performance contracting responds;

- summarizing strengths and weaknesses of performance

contracting as its users have perceived them, and when possible, evaluating these perceptions against subsequent performance;

• defining the roles of third parties and the extent to which they can help school administrators plan, manage, and evaluate a performance contracting program;

• projecting the implications of performance contracting for current and future school system practices and organizations;

• assessing the utility of performance contracting as an alternative mode of resource allocation and making recommendations useful to those planning to engage in a performance contract.

The Papers

The papers included in this volume deal with six different aspects of performance contracting for education:

• *Major Problems in Performance Contracting for Education*, by Donald M. Levine, discusses:

1. measurement, testing, and evaluation problems related to such areas as uncertain affective outcomes, proxy measures, reliable measurement of cognitive outcomes, sub-optimization of the learning program, and learning gain persistence;

2. resource measurement and assessment problems primarily related to the difficulty of discerning the impact of a broad range of inputs upon learning program outcomes; and

3. situational conditions, such as the curricular locus of the performance contract, the characteristics of the student population that will participate, teacher and union relations, school system flexibility, and school system environment.

This paper emphasizes not only the aforementioned areas of concern, but also the social impact of performance contracting and its long term implications for school systems.

• Polly Carpenter's *An Evaluation of Performance Contracting for HEW* summarizes the findings of the Rand performance contracting study team with regard to the efficacy of performance contracting as a technique for solving problems in education. It does not attempt to compare specific programs because of the wide diversity within the programs which were implemented and because of the diversity within the programs themselves. Rather, the effects of performance contracting are discussed in six areas of educational concern: instruction, student learning, evaluation, program management, program cost, and learning system contractors. The major disadvantages and advantages of performance contracting as a technique also are noted.

• The third paper, *Some Problems in Assessing Educational Performance*, by Robert L. Ebel, discusses eight measurement and evaluation issues:

1. The problem of what to assess: performance or capability? Cognitive or non-cognitive learnings? Knowledge or intellectual skills? Attitudes toward and satisfactions in learning?

2. The problem of how to assess it: informal observation or formal testing? Objective or essay tests? Norm-referenced or criterion-referenced tests? Familiar or novel

tests? Motivating the examinee.

3. The problem of too much testing: values and drawbacks of frequent testing. Need for data vs. time devoted to testing.
4. The problem of who should assess it: values and limitations of assessment by contractor, client, outside evaluator, and the students.
5. The problem of obtaining the test: test publisher? Custom made? Test specifications, item writing, pretesting, test authors.
6. The problem of test security: useful and harmful teaching to the test, purloined items or tests and coaching, equivalent new forms.
7. The problem of score interpretation: who is responsible, item proportions or test scores, individual or group scores, sampling errors, gain scores, adjustments for ability.
8. The problem of determining acceptable performance: mastery, minimal proficiency, *a priori* judgment or *a posteriori* data, individual differences.

This paper concludes with recommendations for the future.

• *Program Cost Analysis in Educational Planning*, by Sue A. Haggart, describes a planning cost model and its use in estimating program cost. The model explicitly deals with the problem inherent in using an undefined cost per student as an input for comparing programs.

The model is used to systematically and consistently generate two types of program cost:

1. The comparable replication cost of the program.
2. The cost of the program in a specific district.

The *comparable replication cost* (CRC) is the output of the model that attempts to put the dollar costs of a program in different school districts throughout the country on a *comparable basis*. This means that allowances are made for price differentials and for differences in the use of existing (or surplus) resources available within specific districts. The CRC is, therefore, essentially an *index* or synthetic number to be used only in making interdistrict program cost-effectiveness comparisons.

The model is used to estimate the cost of the program in a specific district by first determining the incremental resources required based on the availability of resources within the district, and then using district-specific prices for the resources. The output of the model, used in this mode, is the estimated cost of a program or alternative programs for the district.

- Selma J. Mushkin's *Performance Toward What Result? An Examination of Some Problems in Outcome Measurement* reviews the approach and tentative findings of a study at the Public Service Laboratory of Georgetown University on statistical measurements of educational outputs. It presents work that has been done on (a) standardization of achievement testing for population characteristics and (b) measurements of the child's perception of self and of society. The noncognitive measures importantly impact on the development of the child and have important consequences for learning, and this paper seeks to assess what can now be done about building affective testing into planning for performance payments.

The findings of the Public Service Laboratory study are presented in summary form with emphasis on the question "What is the relevance of the study's tentative findings to the question of performance?"

- Finally, *Employment Relations Under Performance Con-*

tracting, by Myron Lieberman, discusses seven important aspects of employment relations under performance contracts:

1. What are the actual employment relations under current performance contracts?
2. What is the actual and potential impact of these relationships upon regular school district employment relations?
3. What has been the response of teacher organizations to the specific arrangements providing for performance contracts?
4. To what extent, if any, are performance contracts blocked or modified by teacher attitudes and policies with respect to employment relations in performance contracts?
5. To what extent do performance contracts provide for "merit pay," and how have arrangements for merit pay worked out in practice?
6. To what extent, if any, do teacher-board negotiations deal with performance contracts, e.g., do teachers try to prohibit the contracting out of educational work?
7. What appear to be the main issues and alternative solutions or approaches concerning employment relations in performance contracting and how are they likely to affect the future of performance contracting?

Chapters two through seven present the papers commissioned for the conference. These are followed by post-conference summaries submitted by most of the participants (Chapter Eight).

2.

Major Problems in
Performance Contracting for Education

DONALD M. LEVINE

Introduction

The 1970-1971 academic year brought with it an unprecedented and almost unbalanced surge in the growth of performance contracting for public school systems. In 1969-1970, only one major performance contract for education was fully operational; but in 1970-1971, more than 100 were operational, and many more were in the planning stage.[1] The particular reasons for this growth are manifold, and we shall refer to them later; but, in almost every case, one of two attitudes seems likely to prevail: the participating school system either sees performance contracting as a self-sufficient remedy, as some species of panacea; or it justifies an eagerness to become involved with performance contracting under the heading of experimentation, which lowers the perceived risk of such programs. As Gordon MacAndrew, Superintendent of Schools in Gary, Indiana, put it, "How can we lose?"[2] In both cases there is a great temptation to plunge into performance contracting without due consideration of that technique's applicability to the school system in question. Even granting the "no-penalty" nature of experimentation, this can be a serious error, for a poorly designed performance contracting program can prove financially dangerous, organizationally disruptive, and educationally destructive. It is vital, therefore, to examine problematic aspects of the performance contracting technique in order to determine its general feasibility for education in the future and to explore the situational constraints on its applicability to particular school systems, constraints that will shape our efforts to plan for a performance contracting program. The first two sections of this paper deal with issues connected, respectively, with the problems of measurement, testing, and evaluation and with the problems of resource measurement and impact assessment. The final and major section discusses structural and dynamic school system characteristics that must be considered in planning for a future performance contracting program and seeks to specify preconditions that seem to favor successful implementation of a performance contracting program and to encourage school system receptivity to such an approach.

Because of our lack of long-term experience with performance contracting for education, some of our answers to these questions will be deductive rather than strictly empirical. Yet the theory of performance contracting is sufficiently explicit, and the need to answer these questions sufficiently pressing, to justify some departure from the more restrictive research viewpoint.

Technical Problems

From the viewpoints of both research and practice, the most important issue in performance contracting for education may well be that of measurement, testing, and evaluation. It is important to understand the different purposes for which we evaluate performance, because those purposes affect the kinds of measures and tests we can use. First, and most obviously, we evaluate performance in order to determine contractor payments. The utility of evaluation for this purpose depends at least as much on the payment schedule—which links performance measurement to payment—as it does on the actual measures and tests applied, for the schedule may be adjusted to offset suspected inequities and errors in the tools of measurement. Still, the validity of such tools is the basic problem that has attracted the most critical attention. There are four major criticisms:

1. The standardized tests generally used to determine at least part of the contractor's payment are frequently inappropriate to the contractor's program. Standardized tests designed to measure generalized learnings necessarily ignore the special content and objectives of a particular contracted program as well as other important circumstances affecting program success, from variations in student ability to heterogeneity of test group population. And they are not designed to measure the success of relatively short-term and special purpose programs, such as those involved in most performance contracts. Moreover, such norm-referenced tests are based on imperfectly controlled populations which may differ greatly from the student population being tested, whose scores consequently suffer from cultural and, in some tests, ability bias unrelated to the learning in question.

2. The individual achievement test gain scores often used to compute payments do not reflect actual achievement only. As Stake and Waldrop have put it, gain scores may "assure the appearance of learning where there is no learning at all" because "the conventional achievement test does not have the necessary content validity for individual student assessment."[3] The large proportion of error and low reliability of simple individual gain computed by taking the arithmetic difference of pretest and posttest scores make gain scores a dangerous basis for payments. Some of this danger can be allayed by penalizing the contractor for achievement losses to the same extent he is rewarded for gains, which will average out fortuitous over- and under-payments; by focusing on group gain scores, which should average out errors before payment is made; or by mathematically dropping out a

percentage of error in order to derive "actual" achievement scores. But each of these solutions has its own, mainly operational, drawbacks. (Another, less frequently mentioned, defect of traditional gain scores is that degree of gain correlates closely with the pretest score, but this problem seems more amenable to an explicit, mathematical solution.[4])

3. The grade level increases into which gain scores are translated for payment and publication purposes have all the inadequacies of gain scores but introduce more error because grade level increases measured on different types of tests are not comparable. Thus, grade level increases imply a false degree of certainty, and their very simplification encourages explicit but meaningless comparisons. Grade level increases may have pragmatic advantages, but they are a totally inadequate basis for compensation or for comparative evaluations within and among performance contracting programs.

4. The criterion-referenced tests so frequently mentioned as substitutes for standardized achievement tests have their own defects. They are particularly open to contractor abuses in design and execution and therefore require very careful negotiation and supervision. More importantly, they encourage optimization of limited, myopic, or even irrelevant curricular objectives at the expense of higher program and system goals. The criteria of such tests are not necessarily germane to generally accepted notions of education. This problem might be circumvented if contracting school systems had meaningful goal and objective hierarchies to which they could relate proposed criteria, but most systems are far from this degree of self-consciousness.

This last criticism closely relates to a second purpose of evaluation—to assess the value of the performance contracting program within the school system, to go beyond achievement tests in order to isolate the program's performance against such higher goals as technological innovation and to discern its varied impacts on system structure and personnel. This seems to be the kind of evaluation that the Rand-HEW study stressed, and it is vital to school systems at this experimental stage in the evolution of performance contracting. Clearly, such evaluation should be long-term, since the real utility of performance contracting depends on its ability to effect lasting school system improvements. And it must employ a range of measures within which objective, formalized tests will occupy only a small place. Exactly what mix of measures should be used for program evaluation remains unclear, but it must depend on the school system's particular objectives in deciding to implement performance contracting, and it should include a variety of behavioral measures in order to catch the profound effects of the new roles that this technique imposes on many people and groups within the system. Again, a hierarchy of goals and objectives seems almost indispensable for designing this kind of evaluation.

The aforementioned purposes of evaluation are concerned with output measurement of various kinds; but the third major purpose of evaluation focuses as much on inputs, and this leads us into another group of technical problems—resource measurement and impact assessment. This third purpose is to discriminate among the contributions to program outcomes that are made by the diverse participants in and elements of a performance contracting program. The end of such discrimination is the development of the kinds of input-output models and cost-effectiveness relationships which will permit us to rationally restructure future performance contracting programs and to allocate resources within and among competing programs. It is very difficult to discern the discrete impact of a certain input or resource level upon program outcomes—again, because of outcome measurement difficulties. In this case, though, the ability of the standardized test to measure achievement gains reliably is somewhat irrelevant, for the problem is that most standardized tests are combined measures which lump outcomes together, that do not decompose behavior sufficiently for us to build meaningful models. This problem of combined measures seems technically irreducible in many cases, but it does not actually destroy our ability to derive some idea of the effectiveness of such gross inputs as the technological aspects of the contractor's program or the affective impact of school system personnel. We can use measures other than standardized tests—structured interviews, clinical observation, questionnaires, etc.—to get some feel for the impact of these resources.

Another problem arises when we come to measure the actual resources used in a performance contracting program and attempt to build cost-structures for purposes of comparison and decision-making. The resources consumed may have hidden or sunk costs, or their cost may vary significantly across the country. It can be difficult to separate costs to the contractor from costs to the school system, as it can be to determine precisely what resources should and should not be accounted for. Clearly, this problem hinders cost-effectiveness studies of performance contracting; but it seems more tractable than that of output measurement.

Preconditions

One of the structural preconditions that most influences planning for a performance contracting program is the *curricular locus* of the problems whose solution might call for a performance contracting program. Certain parts of a school system's curriculum are more amenable to performance contracting than other parts, and for rather convincing reasons.[5] The "best" curriculum segment for this technique is vocational education, or any segment that primarily involves training activities. This is because training programs traditionally have objectives that can be accurately stated in concrete, behavioral terms. A reasonable objective of a typing course, for example, might be "to have each student type at 40 words per minute with less than 15 percent error after twenty hours of instruction." Such an objective needs no major redefinition or clarification to serve the purposes of performance contracting—it is sufficiently specific for both parties to know what task must be performed, and it is easy to derive unequivocal performance measures from this objective, thus eliminating the possibility of serious testing—and hence remunerative—distortion. And in cases like this, the frequently dysfunctional practice of "teaching to the test" is precisely what the school system wants.

A much less desirable, but seemingly practicable, curricular locus is basic verbal and quantitative skills. Reading and math objectives are seldom so complete and unequivocal as to preclude debate between contractor and school system about exactly what is to be achieved and how it is to be measured; and third party supervision and/or arbitration often is necessary when the parties to the contract are disputing objectives and performance measures for these basic programs. Yet both educators and contractors have seemed willing to accept a range of surrogate or proxy measures (mainly connected with standardized tests) when negotiating for programs at this level. Such acceptance raises serious and possibly expensive questions about the validity of the performance payment schedule, about sub-optimization, and about the real meaning and persistence of verbal and mathematical achievement.[6] Still, it has provided a mutually held, operational set of objectives, measures, and tests for performance contracting. A major reason for this development, according to our experience to date, is that the need for new, more effective approaches to learning basic verbal and mathematical skills has dictated that most performance contracts—whether integral or experimental (demonstration)—concentrate exclusively on basic reading and math ability. Though these curricular foci are less well suited to the clear definition and measurement of performance that training programs can provide, school administrators have been willing to accept proxies for the sake of whatever solutions performance contracting can find.

The curricular loci that seem least appropriate for a performance contract are those with high normative or affective content. It is hard to pinpoint these loci, since training programs and basic skills programs themselves have significant non-cognitive aspects; but we might look to the curriculum as a whole to have more affective influence than any of its parts. Certainly, the gross curriculum and its more affective loci share the same impediment to performance contracting—highly debatable outputs that generally defy meaningful quantification. It is important to realize that the affective results of a performance contract for *any* curricular locus are questionable, and few efforts have yet been made to define or limit those results. Given the contractor's profit-maximizing behavior, which usually is channeled only by certain cognitive objectives and measures and constrained only by time and resource specifications, a performance contracting program may well have serious, unforeseen affective consequences.[7] Moreover, such change can be unpredictable, and, from the school administrator's point of view, uncontrollable.

A second important precondition is the nature of the school system's student population, and the data the system has collected to describe that population. Data along several relevant dimensions—past performance in school and on "diagnostic" tests, age, length of time within the school system, family background, etc.—may be used to write final contract specifications. Most contractors will insist on such information as a basis for rationally negotiating the limitations of enrollment in the contracted program (unless, of course, the program is school-wide). Such data are particularly important for explicitly experimental contracts, where control of subject (student) characteristics can be essential to subsequent evaluation of the performance contracting program. It would be rash to contend that any particular type of student population inherently favors letting a performance contract, yet most performance contracts to date have involved groups of disadvantaged students. Thus we must ask which characteristics of this kind of population seem to fit particularly well with certain kinds of performance contracts and explore the causes of the prevalence of disadvantaged students as the participants in performance contracting programs.

One obvious cause is that this is a population for which the school system's own methods frequently have failed to produce lasting, significant achievement gains, or even to maintain previous rates of measured achievement growth. In such cases, outside help—especially help that is explicitly motivated to improve student performance—may be indicated as nothing more than a last resort. Second, disadvantaged students often seem to have relatively clear-cut problems, both of academic achievement and of more general behavior. Thus it seems easier to specify objectives for this population and to create fairly homogeneous target groups for operational, experimental, and evaluative purposes. A third apparent cause of the high incidence of disadvantaged students in performance contracting programs is that the problems of this group seem intimately connected with motivation, and performance contractors—who come from the competitive world of business and operate in situations that involve highly motivating incentives—have shown particular strength in designing effective student motivation systems that include a range of extrinsic and intrinsic rewards. The affective by-products of such systems are, indeed, questionable, and they can entail painful issues of pedagogic ethics; yet from the limited viewpoint of effectiveness in cognitive development, at least, they hold promise for the disadvantaged. Finally, there are powerful pragmatic considerations that apparently suit disadvantaged populations to performance contracts. Such populations have attracted increasing attention in the community, as have school system failures to improve their achievement scores. Hence *any* new program for the disadvantaged, and especially one that promises concrete, short-term, highly visible performance gains, is politically attractive and constitutes a powerful community relations tool. Moreover, the presence of federal funds for the disadvantaged tends to encourage school systems to try unproved, experimental programs for that group, and the performance contracting concept builds in the · objective specification, cost structure, and evaluation that federal funding requires. And, in general, many school systems view the use of performance contracting for the disadvantaged as a "no penalty" situation, since they feel that the contractor cannot aggravate and may ameliorate the plight of the disadvantaged.

This analysis of current performance contracting applications cannot tell us that a student population with significant numbers of the disadvantaged is a necessary precondition for a performance contracting program. What it can imply is that positive indications for performance contracting implementation would include a student population or sub-group:

   a.   that has failed to show satisfactory achievement gains in response to school system efforts;
   b.   that has relatively specific problems and characteristics;
   c.   that has apparently low achievement motivation.

A third precondition concerns the school system's teachers and its interactions with them. Organizational climate and culture are important factors here, for teachers will respond to performance contracting largely in the ways the school system has taught them to respond to other innovations and external influences. If in the past the system has cultivated the teachers' achievement motivation by creating a climate which stresses autonomy, professional responsibility, moderately high standards, and specific rewards—either intrinsic or extrinsic—for success, it is probable that teachers will have developed the ability to exploit many factors in their environment for their own—and presumably, their pupils'—success. In the best sense of the word, they will be entrepreneurs—flexible, inventive, and adaptive. In such a case, the school administrator may have little need for a performance contracting program because his in-house levels of achievement are satisfactory; but if he does perceive the need for such a program, he can have some assurance that his personnel will be able to participate creatively in the contractor's program and to take full advantage of it for their own purposes during the turnkey phase. (With a school system like this, the administrator also may want to explore the possibility of so-called "in-house" performance contracting, which is more a control technique than a resource allocation system.) Especially when the contract specifies involvement of school system teachers, as most do, achievement oriented personnel are an excellent precondition for performance contracting; yet the administrator must be careful about introducing the performance contracting concept and the contracted program. Unless he stresses that performance contracting is being used primarily to introduce new technologies and strategies to help teachers improve their effectiveness; that teachers will be involved in planning and operating the performance contracting program; and that the contractor will work closely with teachers, his highly motivated personnel are likely to feel by-passed and unfairly excluded from decisions important enough to merit their participation.

In contrast, a school system whose organizational climate fails to encourage achievement motivation because it emphasizes conformity, risk-aversion, and conflict-avoidance may expect to have teachers concerned primarily with accommodation to the bureaucracy and motivated by considerations of job security. A system-teacher situation of this type is at once most likely to require such techniques as performance contracting in order to improve student achievement, and least likely to be able to implement performance contracting successfully. Although the norm of conformity and the habit of accommodation can elicit token compliance with the performance contracting program, the teachers are likely to view any such innovation as a threat to job security, and hence to resist it staunchly. More importantly, they may be both unwilling and unable to participate effectively in the contracted program (thus aggravating their own perception of job threat), and will tend to welcome the turnkey phase not as an opportunity to acquire a proven teaching technology for their own use, but as the merciful end to a period of high anxiety. In such cases, the administrator may count himself fortunate if performance contracting meets only with teacher apathy and not with more explicit and disruptive types of obstructionism.

Realistically, neither of the above stereotypes will characterize a particular school system; actual organizational climates and teacher attitudes will fall somewhere between these two extremes. The third precondition, then, can be stated as a question of degree: "Do the system and the teachers in question have sufficiently low levels of success to need a performance contracting program and sufficiently high achievement orientations to be able to use one?" If the answer to the second part of this question is negative, the school system probably has a serious teacher motivation problem which performance contracting for student achievement cannot remedy. In this case, performance contracting for teacher training may be indicated.

One other aspect of this precondition demands attention—the generally anti-performance contracting stance of teachers' unions and associations. This resistance is not as uniform as it may seem, for many teachers evidently have been willing to go along with performance contracting, at least in the experimental stage. But where compliance does occur, it must be described as temporary and ultimately dependent on three factors:

    a.   teacher perceptions of performance contracting's threat to tenure, to traditional salary structures, to the prevailing professional-paraprofessional mix, and to the value of certification;

    b.   union resolutions and local strength; and

    c.   legal questions about the necessity of developing performance contracts through collective bargaining.

Union opposition may entail so much conflict and such degeneration of system-teacher relations that the projected value of performance contracting becomes marginal. There are, however, several ways in which school administrators can seek to preclude the development of union opposition and even in some cases to overcome it. First, the group of educational and training techniques that compose the Organizational Development approach can be used to help teachers "own" the performance contracting program and understand it operationally. Second, the program specifications that prospective contractors must meet can be adjusted to reflect teacher concerns about automation (through teaching machines), erosion of professional status (through use of non-certified personnel), job competition (from teachers hired by the contractor outside the system), and other threatening aspects of performance contracting. Third, before contacting potential contractors, the school system can try to sell the concept, not only to teachers and legislators, but to the community as well. And, finally, if the administrator feels that his personnel are sufficiently knowledgeable and motivated to explore new teaching technologies by themselves, he may respond to union opposition by considering so-called "in-house" performance contracts on a competitive, cost-effectiveness basis with external proposals.

A fourth general but very important precondition is the nature of the immediate school system—the structures, personalities, and procedures that directly determine operations in the classroom. This precondition can be divided into at least three major questions:

1. Are current testing procedures sufficiently informative to be used as a basis for selecting potential pupils for the contractor's program? Have they produced a data base reliable enough not only for grouping students, but also for informing the general design and specific objectives of the program to be contracted? And has the school system developed a testing program which inspires enough confidence to permit using it as a determinant of contractor payment? Because diagnostic data and testing are so crucial to the design and operation of a performance contracting program, the school system that already has satisfactory testing procedures is much better suited to performance contracting, and can exercise more effective control over the contractor, than the system that lacks such procedures. Moreover, the difficulty, expense, and danger of developing such procedures within the context of an operational performance contract cannot be overemphasized. Even if the school system seeks to avoid undue contractor influence in the design of testing by arranging with another firm or agency for test development or application (usually at significant cost), the intended use of the testing program may bias its broader validity. The school system that

lacks a previously developed testing program, in addition, will be unable to verify the utility of testing procedures before having to use them in the very sensitive area of payment determination; unable to develop the necessary data base; and unable to negotiate from a position of strength when performance measures are being written into the contract. Clearly, the existence and perceived validity of a data base and testing procedures are a significant precondition, and the school system that lacks such tools is well advised to develop them and gain experience with them before it initiates a performance contracting program.

2. Is the school system sufficiently flexible to adapt to the contractor's program and to take full advantage of it after the turnkey phase? This is a broad question that includes flexibility of student grouping, of classroom scheduling, of teacher utilization, of curriculum composition, and of administrative procedures. These elements are important because the contractor and his program, as intruders in the regular school system, are prone to isolation and ultimate rejection unless they are thoroughly integrated from the start; and since the contractor essentially is free to design whatever program he feels will maximize achievement for his limited group of students, the onus of integration and adaptation during the life of the contract falls on the school system.

The longer term success of a performance contracting program depends on the successful transference of contractor technology. An important determinant of this process is school system flexibility during the turnkey phase, when the system will be required for the first time to assume full responsibility for operating the contracted program. Thus, for the sake of ultimate success, as well as for effective, integrated, short-term operation, the administrator must assess his system's flexibility and explore its limits before he considers performance contracting.

3. A related question is whether the school system is sufficiently aware of its own educational goals, objectives, and programs to envision where a performance contracting program might be productive. Does the system engage in the kinds of operational and strategic planning that will enable it to set goals and objectives for its performance contracting program, to determine appropriate foci for evaluation, and to specify the ways in which performance contracting and its goals are supposed to contribute to higher level system goals and programs? This last issue is crucial because of the familiar danger of sub-optimization, an outcome especially likely with approaches which—like performance contracting—combine great freedom of design and operation with very powerful incentives to achieve. In such cases, the premium placed on performance and the almost unlimited number of alternatives tend to focus attention on the palpability of results, and not so much on the relevance of those results to system goals. Though all the possibly sub-optimal effects of a contractor's program cannot be specified and restricted, the major outputs can be limited to the evidently goal-congruent, and evaluation can be designed to discourage certain kinds of sub-optimization. But the actual ability to develop these limits and to design related evaluation schemes rests on system self-consciousness, a highly variable precondition that often finds explicit statement through planning activities.[8]

Finally, the nature of the larger school system and its environment are significant preconditions for a performance contracting program. Relevant aspects of this precondition include:

1. The contracting authority. As pointed out by the Division of Evaluation of the New York State Education Department,[9] the legal power of a school district to contract for outside services, particularly the extensive instructional services of most perform-

ance contractors, is unclear and varies from state to state. It also varies according to the type of funds used; for, when federal funds are employed, the contracting agency legally is seen as the federal government. But when a federally-initiated performance contracting program eventually is turned over to the school system, the problem of contracting authority re-appears, and it may require special, enabling legislation. In theory, this problem stems from the issues of who is to operate the school system and of the degree to which contracts with third parties constitute abrogations of school system responsibility for educational operations; so, performance contracts that carefully delimit the contractor's authority and emphasize school system responsibility for program results may do much to nullify the legal problem.

2. Resource allocation procedures. Variations in local resource allocation procedures and the relative fiscal influence of the superintendent, the school board, and, in some cases, the city council significantly affect the feasibility of implementing a performance contracting program. If the resource allocation process involves significant political inputs, performance contracting easily can become an issue in factional warfare. In such cases, the respect accorded the superintendent and his professional staff and the degree to which they are the ultimate judges of discretionary expenditures can be decisive. These and other aspects of resource allocation—including the influence on school system policy and finances exercised by an informed, articulate electorate—will do much to affect the initiation, continuation, and disruptiveness of a performance contracting program.

3. Almost equally important are the locally perceived problems and responsibilities of the school system. As opponents of performance contracting have noted, it is possible to view this approach as an abdication of school system responsibility. And the local reputation and history of the school system will largely

dictate whether performance contracting is seen as an evasive tactic or as an attempted improvement by means of expertise and economies of scale in research and development. Similarly, local perceptions of the school system's major problems (whether its weaknesses lie in particular segments of the curriculum, in personnel quality, in accountability, or in some other area) will affect the feasibility of performance contracting and even play some part in which aspects of such a program the school system will emphasize. The combination of all these local views, both within the school system and among the community, ultimately will affect the larger school system's attitude toward performance contracting, and determine if it is to be one of parochialism, which is highly suspicious of the innovation; of cynical cosmpolitanism, which treats it as simply another new approach to student achievement; or one of genuine experimentalism, which is willing to wait for results to corroborate either of the preceding stances.

The long term impact of performance contracting on school systems and on society at large is difficult to predict, for the real ability of this technique to break through the technological and pedagogic barriers of education is still in doubt. It may be that performance contracting will prove to have been simply another blind alley in the search for educational effectiveness. But that seems unlikely.

Whatever its ultimate utility, performance contracting will have confirmed the fact that education need not remain the preserve of the certified professional, that there are alternative methods and alternative personnel who may be, in their own ways, as effective as the trained teacher. And it will have widened the horizons of school administrators by confronting them with organizations whose survival depends on educational efficiency.

If performance contracting for education is to persist, we probably must look for a permanent revolution within the academic profession; for a more militant public that has learned it can ask for and receive seemingly real achievement gains for its children; and for a profound change in the role of the school administrator, who may find himself very quickly transformed from an inspirational leader into a manager of educational services.

Notes

1. J.P. Stucker and G.R. Hall. *The Performance Contracting Concept in Education.* Rand, Santa Monica, California, 1971, pp. 25-29.
2. *Globe and Mail*, Toronto, Canada, November 18, 1971, p. W-6.
3. Robert E. Stake and James L. Waldrop. Gain Score Errors in Performance Contracting, a paper presented to the American Educational Research Association, February 1971.
4. See Robert A. Feldmesser. Tests and the ETS Role in Performance Contracting, a paper internally circulated at Educational Testing Service.
5. See Stucker and Hall, *The Performance Contracting Concept in Education*, p. 11.
6. If the contract negotiators have fairly accurate perceptions of the linkage between "real" performance (what the system actually wants) and measures like "grade equivalence," of course, they have a better chance of producing an effective performance contract. But the defects of grade equivalence render such perceptions rare.
7. A case in point is modification of student behavior—and achievement of contract objectives—through an extrinsic reward system.
8. The task of developing such awareness may not be as forbidding as it seems, for most school system members thoroughly comprehend system goals without having for-

malized them. The problem then becomes one of heightening a pre-existing awareness, frequently through rather simple goal-setting processes.

9. The University of the State of New York, The State Education Department, *Performance Contracting in Elementary and Secondary Education,* Albany, December 1970, pp. 4, 9, and 24.

3.

An Evaluation of Performance Contracting for HEW

POLLY CARPENTER

Introduction

Performance contracting is a very controversial concept. It implies involving profit-oriented firms in public school classroom duty. It also implies using test results to measure the effectiveness of instruction and to measure educational output. Both these features have produced extensive interest and concern, not only among the educators but among the general public as well. The history of performance contracting has been evident in popular magazines, the press, and television.

Local educational officials have expressed the need for materials which would assist them in deciding about performance contracting programs for their districts. The U.S. Department of Health, Education, and Welfare, in the summer of 1970, decided to sponsor the preparation of a guide to meet this need. Rand was asked by HEW officials to undertake the project, which ended early in 1972.

Because any guide should be firmly grounded in empirical study of actual programs, we monitored in depth, eight programs in five cities. We also followed, in less detail, about 15 other

Polly Carpenter is with the education group in the System Sciences Department of The Rand Corporation, Santa Monica, California.

programs or attempts to get programs under way. The results of Rand's work were presented in three reports available to the public. The first report is *The Performance Contracting Concept in Education.* The second is *Case Studies in Performance Contracting.* The third and final report is *The Performance Contracting Guide* addressed to decision-makers in local school districts.

HEW officials were very perceptive forecasters when in 1970 they predicted that performance contracting would be a very popular innovation. Why the popularity? There are probably two major reasons for the great interest in performance contracting. The first is that business firms have been asserting that they have the technology and skills to close the achievement gap between students from economically poor homes and those from more advantaged environments. Those in the field of education have been wrestling with America's compensatory education problems for some years with heartbreaking results. They are ripe to respond to any promise of help. A second reason for the popularity of performance contracting has been a hope that it might be an agent for change. Education is a field within which there has been a relatively low rate of innovation. Any mechanism that might overcome the barriers to new techniques or technology is very attractive. In short, then, in addition to examining an intriguing new relationship between public and private organizations, the Rand-HEW study dealt with some very basic issues of educational policy: *the problem of improving compensatory education and that of stimulating innovation.*

The Rand-HEW Study

Many people contributed to our field evaluation of ongoing performance contracting programs. They represented a variety of disciplines—not only education, but mathematics, economics, business administration, and psychology. Our approach was, first, to choose a few programs to study extensively so that we would really understand what was going on. At the same time, we wanted the sample to be diverse enough to permit us to generalize the conclusions that we formed. We also knew that we needed a flexible plan because the programs would change as the year progressed. Finally, we used a variety of data-gathering techniques: questionnaires, interviews of students, teachers and prominent people in the community, observation in the contracted classrooms and in regular classrooms, searches of records in central files and in school files, and, in some cases, administration of special tests to program students.

The cities in which we did our work represented geographically varied areas: Gilroy, California, the far west; Texarkana, Arkansas, the south central region; Gary, Indiana, and Grand Rapids, Michigan (industrial cities), the northeastern region; and Norfolk, Virginia (a southern city) on the eastern seaboard. Not only were these cities geographically varied, their other characteristics were varied also. Population ranged from quite small in Gilroy (around 11,000) to fairly large in Norfolk (around 300,000). School enrollments ranged from 5,000 in Gilroy to 55,000 in Norfolk. The predominant minority group in each city was usually black, although in Gilroy the minority group was Spanish surnamed. The percent of minority was also quite varied; as a matter of fact the 60 percent "minority" in Gary indicates that the blacks are actually the majority in that particular city.

The programs themselves also were quite diverse. Some of the major features of the eight programs studied are displayed in Figure 1. The contractors were Behavioral Research Laboratories in Gary; Westinghouse Learning Corporation in Gilroy and in Grand Rapids; Alpha Learning Systems in Grand Rapids (Alpha was part of the OEO experiment), CMES (Combined Motivation and Education Systems) in Grand Rapids; Learning Research

Figure 1

Features of the Eight Programs

City Name	Contractor	Subjects	Students	Grades	Contractor Selection*	Contract Management Support	Contract Evaluation or Audit
Gary	BRL	All	850	K-6	S	No	Yes
Gilroy	WLC	Reading, Math	100	2-4	S	No	No
	Alpha	Reading, Math	600	1-3, 7-9	C	Yes	Yes
Grand Rapids	CMES	Reading, Math	600	6-9	S	No	Yes
	WLC	Reading, Math	400	1-6	S	No	No
Norfolk	LRA	Reading	150	4-9	C	Yes	Yes
Texarkana	Dorsett (1969-1970)	Reading, Math	350	7-12	C	Yes	Yes
	EDL (1970-1971)	Reading, Math	285	7-12	C	Yes	Yes

* S = sole source selection
C = competitive bid selection

Associates in Norfolk; and Dorsett Educational Systems (during 1969-1970) and Educational Development Laboratories, a division of McGraw-Hill (during 1970-1971), in Texarkana.

The subjects taught were generally reading and mathematics, although in Norfolk reading was the only subject taught. In Gary, all subjects in the curriculum were taught, since Gary's program involved the entire Banneker Elementary School. Unlike most experimental and demonstration programs in education, most of these programs involved fairly large numbers of students. The Gilroy program was the smallest with only 100 students; the Gary program, the largest with 850. Grades ranged from kindergarten to the 12th grade.

Contractors were selected in one of two ways: by sole source (S) selection (that is, the school district agreed beforehand to give the contract to a particular contractor) or by competitive (C) bid (that is, several contractors submitted proposals from which the school district selected one). The programs were evenly divided between those two methods. There were other contractual arrangements. For example, a management support group was often hired to assist the school district in management expertise necessary to handle the business relationships involved in contracts of this type. Similarly, independent evaluation or audit were sometimes contracted on the theory that if an independent evaluator were used, there would be no grounds for charges of collusion. These kinds of arrangements introduced some difficulties in the programs, which will be discussed later.

Effects of Performance Contracting

The effects of performance contracting will be discussed in five areas: instruction, student learning, program cost, program management, and the contractors. Several points will be addressed regarding instruction. Did the programs actually change instruction? What kinds of changes took place? And what was the extent of these changes?

The kinds of changes can best be exemplified in a description of the more open classrooms in the programs. The typical scene in a regular classroom in the inner-city schools had the teacher at the head of the class before rows of students seated in desks bolted to the floor. The teacher might be leading a discussion, asking questions or reprimanding the students. This scene was quite familiar to most of those conducting the study.

The scene in the more open classroom of the performance contracting programs was entirely different. We saw the teacher sitting at a desk, possibly discussing a piece of work with a student; in other parts of the room some students might be sitting at a table, listening to a tape recorder; others would be sitting in study carrels working on workbooks; others sitting at tables reading; and still others walking about getting materials or putting them away. Frequently there would be a teacher aide helping some of the students with their work or with equipment. The contrast with the atmosphere of the regular classroom was quite marked. Students in performance contracting programs seemed to be more self-reliant, more interested in what was going on, more mature about their learning than were the students in regular classrooms.

Another change was that all of the programs emphasized individualization of instruction in the sense that each student was tested to determine his strengths and weaknesses in the program subjects and then a course of study was prescribed tailored to remedy his weaknesses and to build on his strengths. Thus every student could have a slightly different course of study.

There was an emphasis on teaching the skills of reading and mathematics for two reasons. First, these are the skills that almost everyone agrees are necessary for functioning in our technological world, and it is precisely in these skills that the disadvantaged student is weak. Second, it is easier for educators to agree on the precise skills that everyone should have than it is to agree on what should be the content of, say, a social studies curriculum. In effect, reading and mathematics are less controversial subjects than some others that might be taught.

It took time to implement the changes in instruction even within the program, since all of the "learning systems" had to be tailored to fit the many different variables in specific districts. Some of the programs did not become fully implemented until almost half of the year was gone. At the beginning of the study we were also concerned that the programs would remain "encapsulated" the way so many experimental and demonstration programs do in education—a situation where practically nobody outside of the program cares or even knows anything about it. Although this seemed to be the case at the beginning of the 1970-1971 school year, as time went on the programs seemed to be almost selling themselves. Teachers became interested in them, and wanted to know more about the techniques. By the end of the programs, in most cases, the ideas had spread to other teachers and schools in the district. In some instances, teachers who were initially hostile were won over, especially as they began to see that the contractors were not going to be as spectacularly successful as they had first claimed.

The key question, however, is: Did performance contracts have better than average effects on student learning as measured by standardized* tests? The measure used was the gain score—the difference between a student's score on a pretest and his score on

---

*A standardized test is one that has been given to a large number of students throughout the United States so that the test publishers can say what score the average 3rd, 5th, or 6th grade child, for example, will make. A certain student's score may then be compared with these norms to determine his grade level.

a posttest. Normally we would expect that an average student would gain one year in one year of instruction measured, say, in the spring of one year and the spring of the next. However, in these programs this rarely happened, as shown in Figure 2. In Gilroy the reading gain was significantly better than that of other Title I students* that year. The math gain was mixed—better at one grade and worse at another. Since Westinghouse Learning Corporation had promised that the Gilroy program would provide better than one year's growth in one year, the program did not live up to the contractor's promise. The Westinghouse Learning Corporation program in Grand Rapids was similar to that in Gilroy; the gains were about the same as those of the Title I students in Grand Rapids in the past.

The CMES program in Grand Rapids seems to have done quite well. However, the gains made are based on results from only a third of the student population. Frequently in performance contracting programs, contract provisions are not included for students who enter late, or leave early, or who do not have pretest or posttest scores. Only a third of the students in the CMES program took the full course of study and had both pretest and posttest scores. We do not know what the other students would have scored.

The data on the Dorsett Educational Systems (in Texarkana) program will never be available because of the alleged teaching of test items in the Dorsett program. This illustrates an important point. In performance contracting, data may be withheld from the public for various reasons.

In Norfolk we have an interesting situation. At the 7th and

---

*Referring to Title I of the Elementary and Secondary Education Act; these are students that are disadvantaged in terms of various measures such as family income or membership in a minority group.

9th grade levels the students achieved about what they would have achieved in an ordinary program; thus Learning Research Associates did not fulfill its guarantee of 1.7 years of growth in 1 year.

Figure 2

Mean Gains on Standardized Tests

City Name	Contractor	Mean Gains	Remarks
Gary	BRL	1.7/1.7	Reading/Math/1st grade
		.7/1.2	Reading/Math/2nd-6th grade
Gilroy	WLC	.6/ .8	Reading/Math
Grand Rapids	ALPHA	NR	Test Identification not Released by OEO. Three Tests Used.
	CMES	1.2/1.0	Reading/Math
	WLC	.7/ .6	Reading/Math
Norfolk	LRA	0.1	Reading/5th grade
		0.5	Reading/7th grade
		0.5	Reading/9th grade
Texarkana	Dorsett	NR	
	EDL	.5/ .3	Reading/Math/6th-12th grade

At the 5th grade the gain scores appeared to be almost purely the result of chance. The pretest of these students showed many of them to be functionally illiterate, so the teacher chose first to improve their word-attack skills, that is, their ability to hear a word and then find it on the printed page. For most of the year this objective was pursued, and almost none of the children progressed to reading comprehension objectives. But word-attack skills were not included on the norm-referenced (standardized) tests. For example, the Metropolitan Achievement Test (MAT) has three sections, one of which measures word-attack skills. Since this section has to be administered orally, it is expensive to administer and requires special training of test administrators. Thus this section was not used in the evaluation. The two sections used measured reading comprehension and vocabulary. Therefore it is not too surprising that the gain scores on the MAT appeared to be random. (Gain scores on the other two tests used at the 5th grade showed similar distributions.) A test of the word-attack skills assigned to the students in the program showed that they had mastered *these* objectives at the rate of about 80 to 90 percent. We cannot, however, conclude that the students learned something from the program, because they were not pretested on these objectives nor was a control group used. Thus, *in evaluating programs it is necessary that the program and the testing instruments are synchronized and that base-line data are obtained.*

The Gary program appears to have been much more successful than the others, particularly in the area of mathematics. There were two obvious differences between the Gary program and the others. Perhaps the most important was that, because the contractor had control of the *entire* curriculum, he was able to concentrate almost exclusively on teaching reading and math during the first semester. Another important difference was that Gary parents were clearly deeply involved in their children's education, in contrast to most of the parents of students in other programs.

The costs of the performance contracting programs can be compared to each other and to those of other compensatory programs if the unit costs are the same, for example, if a teacher is assumed to receive the same salary whether he or she is teaching in Gary or Norfolk. On this basis, the costs that would be incurred yearly for instruction for reading or mathematics (there was no significant difference in cost between reading and mathematics) of the performance contracting programs would be similar to or sometimes 25 percent less than those of the regular Title I programs. This is because the contractors substituted materials, aides, and equipment for teachers. For example, in the Norfolk performance contracting program the teacher handled 25 students in the classroom, five periods a day. In a comparable remedial-reading program under Title I in Norfolk, the teacher handled 10 students five to six periods a day. Moreover, when we asked the Norfolk teachers in the performance contracting program whether they felt the class size was too large, they said they thought it was too small. They could have handled more students if the room had been larger.

Compensatory programs, including performance contracting programs, should be and are more expensive than regular programs by 60 to 70 percent. After all, these programs are trying to make up for deficiencies not only in the student's education but in his home environment as well.

Performance contracting had an effect on program management. We know that not only school systems but almost all institutions are short of the management talent that is needed to effectively implement change. Fortunately, in each of the programs there was someone willing and able to take over the duties of effectively implementing the program; in some other programs lack of leadership resulted in ineffective implementation. Because the programs were developmental in nature, flexibility of management was needed. There were times when the contractual arrangements actually hindered changes that should have been made to make the program more effective.

Although we would expect qualified teachers to be involved in programs of this type, some of the contractors felt that they had programs that were "teacher-proof" and even went so far as to try to show that no matter what kinds of teachers were assigned, the program would work. By the end of the year, however, these contractors had realized the importance of making use of the teachers' knowledge of the student population as a valuable resource in implementing their programs.

A number of people in the school district had to assume new roles. In order for the contractors to make good their claims that their systems could teach, they had to actually become involved in the instructional process. School administrators had to be sure that they lived up to the terms of the contract: that enough students were available at the right time, that the rooms were ready, and that tests were administered properly. And teachers had to become managers of instruction rather than presenters of information.

What advantages did the contractors receive from their programs? We are not sure that they made any money. None of them fulfilled the performance guarantee except BRL and CMES, but because we do not know how much the 1970-1971 programs actually cost the contractors, we cannot say whether they gained or lost. Although monetary gain has been publicized as one of the reasons contractors are interested in performance contracting, we think they are much more interested in obtaining new markets and follow-on contracts. Most of the contractors have small organizations that have had difficulty breaking into the educational field or providing competition to major textbook manufacturers. The performance contracting mechanism gave them a way in because of the performance guarantee. Follow-on contracts have resulted from almost every program that we have monitored. Westinghouse Learning Corporation in Gilroy is the only one without a follow-on contract because Westinghouse has decided to close down its Learning Division. However, even in Gilroy teachers want to continue the Westinghouse approach in their own learning centers. The demise of Westinghouse in Grand Rapids was followed by the formation of a company called Learning Unlimited, which is going to continue the Westinghouse type of operation.

Advantages and Disadvantages

Performance contracting has some disadvantages and problems. The disadvantages are complexity and narrowness. The technique is inherently complex because the contractual arrangement introduces new problems in assignment of authority and responsibility, and the management of the new program becomes more involved. The technique is currently narrow because the performance contract must focus on skill areas, since the definition of objectives and the construction of tests are difficult in more controversial subjects such as art or social studies.

There was also an exacerbation of old problems. Management problems may be accentuated; legal difficulties may arise from contractual arrangements, which may sometimes violate the education code or agreements with textbook manufacturers or teachers' unions; problems related to tests and test administration will be more obvious because measurement is so crucial to performance contracting; finally, the issue of teacher status has caused difficulty with teachers and teachers' unions.

Performance contracting offers two important advantages for

teachers and students. First, it really does facilitate radical change. Outsiders to the educational system are freer to implement change than are those who are part of the system. Second, performance contracting has caused an increased emphasis on accountability: the schools now feel they are accountable for student learning, rather than for inputs, such as the teacher/student ratio or teachers' salaries. The emphasis on student learning is a very healthy thing. It has forced the contractors to look very carefully at their systems and to understand what their claims mean in terms of student learning. School administrators have become more aware of the problems of evaluation and testing. Teachers have become more aware of the necessity for their students to measure up to other students or to their own past performance; and the students themselves may become accountable in the future. In fact, rumor has it that some students in a small town in Texas complained that, since they were the ones ultimately responsible for their own learning, a performance contract let to a nearby educational firm should have been given to them directly.

In conclusion, we think performance contracting will continue for at least a few years, in spite of some of the poor showings on student achievement. Certainly the follow-on contracts suggest this, even though some of them do not have performance guarantees, and new contractors are entering the field. Performance contracting is also a helpful change agent and does provide the emphasis on accountability that is currently in vogue. Whether the technique will have any lasting benefit we cannot say. First, considerable work will be needed to develop measuring instruments before performance contracting can be of wider use.

The research strategy employed by Rand in the study reported in this chapter is explained in Appendix C, pages 183-185.

4.

Some Problems in Assessing Educational Performance

ROBERT L. EBEL

Background and Overview

The assessment of performance is as old as human history. The last verse of the first chapter of the Book of Genesis says, "And God saw everything that he had made, and behold it was very good." Since then, most of us who were made in His image have had many occasions to follow His good example, though often without the same satisfying conclusion.

Assessing the educational attainments of students, directly, and thus of their teachers, indirectly, also has a long history. It began at least 4,000 years ago, for there are good records of an elaborate system of achievement examinations, which provided entry to the civil service, in the Shun dynasty of ancient China. It continued in the middle ages. The Jesuits, for example, prepared a detailed and technically sophisticated set of rules for the conduct of written examinations which, if followed carefully, would improve many of the examinations we give today.

Assessment played an important role in the early development of public education in this country, at the initiative of Horace Mann and others. It began to become a science, or at least

Robert L. Ebel is Professor of Education and Psychology at Michigan State University.

a technology, in the early years of this century, in the hands of men like Cattell, Thorndike, McCall, and Wood. Now, with the proliferation of wide scale testing programs, with the perfection of electronic test processing equipment, and with public pressure for accountability in the educational enterprise, assessment continues to play a leading role in the process of education. Surely it is an essential part of any system of performance contracting.

The process of assessing performance in education, however, is much more complicated than it appears to be to many of our fellow citizens. As they see it, all one has to do is to give a test. Each student either passes or fails it. The proportion that passes indicates the effectiveness of the educational program. Where the test comes from, what it really measures, how good it is, what the scores mean, how the passing score is determined; these and many other hard questions that trouble test specialists a great deal trouble the general public hardly at all. They trust our technical competence to do the job that needs doing far more than it ought to be trusted. For even among educational specialists there are confusions, uncertainties and sharp differences of opinion. There are, in short, some difficult problems in assessing performance adequately.

This paper is addressed to some of the more important of the problems. It is organized around seven questions which pose the problems:

- What performance should be assessed?
- How should performance be assessed?
- Who should assess educational performance?
- How can the necessary tests be obtained?
- How can teaching to the test be prevented?
- How should the test scores be interpreted?
- What level of performance should be considered satisfactory?

Clearly these problems of assessment are not unique to perform-ance contracting. They arise whenever a performance that can be learned is to be assessed. But some of them have unique facets, or present unusual difficulties, when fulfillment or non-fulfillment of a performance contract is at stake. These special problems will be taken note of as the more general problems are being considered.

**What Performance Should
Be Assessed?**

A direct answer to this question is: "The performance you've been trying to teach." But this answer is not as simple or as obviously correct as it seems at first glance. Some would deny that schools should be concerned primarily with teaching pupils to perform. They would argue that schools should aim to develop the pupil's knowledge, understanding, attitudes, interests, and ideals; that schools should be concerned with cognitive capabilities and affective dispositions rather than with performances. They would agree that capabilities and dispositions can only be assessed by observing performances, but would insist that the performances themselves are not the goals of achievement, but only the *indicators* of it. A teacher who is concerned with the pupil's cognitive capabilities and affective dispositions will teach quite differently, they claim, than one whose attention is focused solely on the pupil's performance. And, if performances are not goals but only indicators, we should choose the ones to use in assessment on the basis of their effectiveness as indicators. Clearly we cannot choose them in terms of the amount of effort we made to develop them.

But, if we reject performance goals, another question arises. What should be the relative emphasis placed on affective disposi-tions as opposed to cognitive capabilities? Here is another issue that divides professional educators. To some, how the pupil feels;

his happiness, his interest, his self-concept, his yearnings are what
should concern teachers the most. To others the pupil's cognitive
resources and capabilities are the main concern. Both would agree
that cognition and affect interact, and that no school ought to
concentrate solely on one and ignore the other. But, they disagree
on which should receive primary emphasis.

In trying to resolve this issue it may be helpful to observe
two things. The first is that the instructional programs of almost
all schools are aimed directly at the cultivation of cognitive
competence in such things as reading, mathematics, written
expression, science, history, etc. The pupil's affective dispositions—his interests, attitudes, self-concept, ideals, etc.—constitute
conditions that facilitate or inhibit cognitive achievement. They
may be enhanced by success or impaired by failure. The rules of
discipline and order adopted and enforced in the school, the
models of excellence and humanity provided by the teachers—
these and other conditions in the school have powerful affective
influences on pupils. But they are by-products, not the main
products of the instructional effort. It is almost impossible to find
any school that has planned and successfully operated an
instructional program aimed primarily at the attainment of
affective goals.

The second thing to observe and remember is that if a school
should set out deliberately to develop certain affective dispositions, it has only two effective means to use. One is the cultivation
of cognitive competence, of knowledge of good and evil, of
consequences likely to follow certain acts. The other is conditioning, the use of rewards and punishments to habituate students to
seek this and avoid that. Conditioning is a powerful tool. Hitler
and his colleagues used it with great success in Germany,
particularly in the Hitler Youth groups. But, clearly, it is also a
dangerous tool. The cultivation of cognitive competence is far

better suited to the education of intelligent beings for life in a free society. Hence, we conclude that the emphasis most schools do place on the cultivation of cognitive competence is not misplaced.

What is cognitive competence? Two distinctly different answers have been given. One is that it requires acquisition of knowledge. The other is that it requires development of intellectual skills. Here is another issue on which educational specialists are divided.

To avoid confusion or superficiality on this issue it is necessary to be quite clear on the meanings attached to the terms *knowledge* and *intellectual skills*. Knowledge, as the term is used here, is not synonymous with information. It is more nearly synonymous with *understanding*. Knowledge is built out of information by thinking. It is an integrated structure of relationships among concepts and propositions. A teacher can give his students information. He cannot give them knowledge. A student must earn the right to say, "I know," by his own thoughtful efforts to understand.

Whatever a person experiences directly in living or vicariously by reading or listening can become part of his knowledge. It will become part of his knowledge if he succeeds in integrating that experience into the structure of his knowledge, so that it makes sense, is likely to be remembered, and will be available for use when needed. Knowledge is essentially a private possession. Information can be made public. Knowledge cannot. Hence, it would be more appropriate to speak of a modern day "information explosion" than of a knowledge explosion.

The term *intellectual skills* has also been used with a variety of meanings. Further, those who use it often do not say, precisely and clearly, what they mean by it. Most of them seem not to mean skill in specific operations, such as spelling a word, adding two fractions, diagramming a sentence or balancing a chemical equation. They are likely to conceive of intellectual skills in much broader terms, such as observing, classifying, measuring, communicating, predicting, inferring, experimenting, formulating hypotheses, and interpreting data.

It seems clear that these broader intellectual skills cannot be developed or used very effectively apart from substantial bodies of relevant knowledge. To be skillful in formulating hypotheses about the cause of a patient's persistent headaches one needs to know a considerable amount of neurology, anatomy and physiology, as much as possible about the known disorders that cause headaches, and a great deal about the history and habits of the person who is suffering them. That is, to show a particular intellectual skill a person must possess the relevant knowledge. (Note well at this point that a person cannot look up the knowledge he needs, for knowledge, in the sense of the term we are using, cannot be looked up. Only information can be looked up. Knowledge has to be built by the knower, himself.) And, if he does possess the relevant knowledge, what else does he need to show the desired skill?

Intellectual skill that goes beyond knowledge can be developed in specific operations like spelling a word or adding fractions. But, the more general (and variable from instance to instance) the operation becomes, the less likely it is that a person's intellectual skill will go far beyond his knowledge.

Those who advocate the development of intellectual skills as the principal cognitive aim of education often express the belief (or hope) that these skills will be broadly transferrable from one area of subject matter to another. But, if the subjects are quite different, the transfer is likely to be quite limited. Who would hire a man well trained in the measurement of personal characteristics for the job of measuring stellar distances and compositions?

Our conclusion at this point is that schools which emphasize cognitive achievements, which is the vast majority of them, should continue to cultivate knowledge rather than something other than knowledge, called intellectual skill. They should continue to do so at least until intellectual skills have been more clearly defined, and their contributions to effective performance which are different from and independent of knowledge have been positively identified.

How Should Performance Be Assessed?

Two small questions and one large one arise when we begin to consider how a learner's educational performance should be assessed. Let us take up the small ones first.

Should performance be assessed by observing the learner's behavior in natural everyday situations or in the somewhat artificial circumstances of a formal test? If we had enough skilled observers so that individual learners could be followed and observed closely as they worked their way through the everyday situations they encounter, if we could get funds to pay for such extensive observation, and if the learner would continue to behave naturally in the presence of the observer, then the first alternative might be worth consideration. But, natural behavior is troublesome and costly to observe systematically, and most difficult to assess precisely. Hence, assessment via testing is almost always preferred, because of its convenience and uniformity and because of the reliability of the assessments it yields. When educational achievements of the kind schools spend most of their time developing are to be assessed, the error introduced by the artificiality of the testing situation tends to be small.

If tests are to be used, should they be essay or objective? If one wishes to assess the quality of a student's prose style, or of his handwriting, the use of an essay test is indispensable. But, if one wishes to assess his structure of knowledge in an area, the objective test can do the job just as adequately, or more so, at the cost of much less time, labor, and money. Objective tests need not be, and seldom are, in fact, limited to testing superficial recall of factual information. Little blind guessing is done on appropriate objective tests by well-motivated examinees. The folklore that disdains objective testing dies hard, but it is clear that such tests provide the only practical means of obtaining valid assessments of performance on any large scale. Education in America is a large-scale operation.

Consider now the larger question that relates to the *how* of assessment. Should the tests be designed to yield norm-referenced or criterion-referenced measures? A criterion-referenced test is intended to indicate how much of some desired achievement a given student has managed to acquire. A norm-referenced test is intended to indicate how the amount one student has acquired compares with the amounts other students have acquired.

It may be useful to note, at this point, that the score on any achievement test can have both criterion-referenced and norm-referenced meaning. That is, it can indicate what proportion of a set of tasks of a given kind a given pupil can successfully complete. If scores of other pupils on the same test are available, the same score can be used to determine where he stands in the group; high, middle or low. Both indicators are useful to the assessor. The issue before us, then, is not whether one kind of meaning should be attended to exclusively, and the other disregarded. It is whether we should build tests so as to be most effective in providing criterion-related or norm-related meaning. Making a test do one of the two jobs better is likely, at least in theory, to make it do the other somewhat less well.

The key to the theoretical difference between the two kinds of tests is in the standards used to select the items. For a criterion-related test each item should be written so that a correct answer indicates attainment of some important element of achievement in the subject of the test. That the item may be answered correctly by most examinees, and, hence, discriminate poorly (by the usual measures of item discrimination) is of little concern. To the constructor of a criterion-referenced test, the relevance of the item to the goals of achievement is more important than the information it provides on differences in achievement among students. This is the theory, at least.

The constructor of a norm-referenced test is also concerned with the relevance of the question to the goals of instruction. But, in addition, he is likely to pay attention to how much information the item provides about differences among pupils in achievement. Given two items of nearly equal relevance to the goals of instruction, he will choose the one that discriminates better between students of high and low achievement. The constructor of the criterion-referenced test would be expected to discount evidence of discriminatory power and choose the item which seemed the more relevant to the goals of instruction.

On closer examination the theoretical differences between norm-referenced and criterion-referenced tests turn out to be less than might appear at first. Relevance, as we have noted, is important in both tests. So is discrimination, despite disclaimers from proponents of criterion-referenced testing. For the items in a criterion-referenced test must discriminate those who have attained a particular goal from those who have not. Both kinds of tests require good test items for which answers (1) can be defended as correct, (2) are not concealed from capable students by ambiguity or inaccuracy of expression, and (3) are not given away to the incapable by unintentional clues. A good criterion-referenced test might be remarkably similar to a good norm-referenced test on the same subjects. With labels removed even a competent judge might find it difficult to tell which was which, just by looking at the items.

Preference for criterion-referenced tests is often based on two rather unrealistic assumptions or expectations. One is that in a well-taught course most of the students will attain most of the objectives of instruction. If they do, even a good test item would show little discrimination among students, for no important differences among them exist to be discriminated. But individual differences among students in background, motivation, and achievement cannot be abolished by Procrustean techniques of "mastery learning," though they may be obscured by repeated testing until a satisfactory performance is attained. Even a homogeneous group of students, when faced with a challenging course of instruction, is likely to show substantial individual differences in achievement. Good items testing that achievement are likely to discriminate between individuals of high and of low achievement.

A second unrealistic assumption is that by basing each item in the test on a separate important objective of instruction, the constructor of a criterion-referenced test can obtain scores that more accurately indicate how much a student has actually learned of what was set out to be learned. The trouble with this notion is that different objectives are not separate, discrete entities, independent of each other. They are all interdependent parts of a complex whole. They tend to resist clear definition as distinct components, for they overlap and interact. Success on a particular discrete test item almost never indicates that one particular discrete objective, and only that objective, has been attained.

"Amount to be learned" and "amount a given student has learned" are both very difficult to quantify precisely. It is usually safe to infer that the student who answers more questions right on the test has learned more about the subject matter of the test than the student who answers fewer questions correctly. But, except in a few special cases, like spelling or the basic addition facts, it is inappropriate to use a test score, even a criterion-referenced test score, as a basis for estimating the fraction a student has learned of what it was hoped he might learn. To make matters worse, the hoped-for amount of learning is usually based on the private subjective judgment of a particular teacher or test constructor. Seldom, if ever, is it based on a generally accepted, clearly defined standard of achievement.

From these considerations we conclude that criterion-referenced testing offers no great promise for substantial improvements in the assessment of educational performance. Test scores need to indicate, and most test scores do indicate, both how much a student has achieved relative to the subject matter and how much he has achieved relative to his classmates or peers. Where we can make those indications more precise or more valid we should do so. But, we should not expect criterion-referenced testing to express the complexity of educational achievement with high precision on a simple numerical scale.

Who Should Assess Educational Performance?

In the educational systems of the United States, student performance has usually been assessed by the person who tried to develop the performance capability, that is by the teacher. Efforts of educational leaders, governmental agencies or the public to introduce external assessments of performance have been strongly resisted by school administrators and classroom teachers. They have justified their opposition on these grounds among others:

- External evaluations of achievement will lead inevitably to external control of the curriculum;

- Externally produced tests are not completely relevant to the local instructional objectives, and hence lead to invalid evaluations;
- Teachers, threatened by possibly unfavorable assessments, will abandon effective pupil-oriented teaching and instead teach to the tests via rote learning and drill; and
- External tests place too much emphasis on easily measured but less essential outcomes, i.e., recall of factual information, to the neglect of more important but less tangible outcomes in the area of personality, adjustment, character and values.

There is some truth, but much more error, in these allegations. External assessments can be harmful to the process of education, but they need not be. Properly employed, they can do much more good than harm. Teachers and school administrators need to face the fact that external evaluation of their effectiveness is inevitable. They cannot escape accountability to students, parents, and taxpayers. The question of external evaluation is not whether but how, and how much, and by whom.

Both the process and the product of education need to be evaluated. The process can be evaluated informally by students, parents, supervisors, and teachers, and formally by specifically designated teams of observers. The product can also be evaluated informally on the basis of incidental observation, or formally on the basis of test performance. It is the use of tests in assessing the product of education that is of most concern to us here.

Who should make the test? Even for an external evaluation the test should be planned by a team including both local teachers and outside evaluation specialists. The test should then be developed externally and administered to pupils by someone other than their regular teacher. Relevance, expertness, and impartiality are the keys to effective external assessment via tests of student performance. The tests used must be relevant to the goals of instruction. The tests should be developed or selected by experts in the measurement of educational achievement. The tests should be administered and scored, and the results interpreted, by persons who have no responsibility for developing the performance which is being assessed.

Important as it is, external assessment provides only part of the information needed for a comprehensive formal assessment of performance. The other main part should come from the teachers themselves, using tests they have designed and built, or selected from available standardized instruments. A balanced program of formal assessment will include both internal and external tests.

What has been said in the preceding paragraphs about assessments of the process and product of education in conventional instruction applies with even greater force in performance contracted instruction. Relevance, expertness, and impartiality are again the keys to success. They also present difficult problems. Because performance contractors seldom have tenure, they are likely to be even more concerned than teachers typically are to have their methods and results assessed fairly and adequately. Because of the money and special effort involved, the school authorities likewise have a large stake in the quality of the assessment. Failure to do a competent, comprehensive job of assessment could discredit the whole enterprise of performance contracting. Doing a competent job is not easy, but it is clearly possible.

How Can the Necessary Tests Be Obtained?

The two obvious alternative answers to this question are (1) to find, select, and buy a satisfactory ready-made standardized test, or (2) to develop or employ someone else to develop a satisfactory custom-made test, built to particular specifications. There are pros and cons to each alternative.

The easy availability, relatively low cost and good repute of a widely used standardized test are persuasive arguments for the first alternative. Furthermore, published standardized tests are usually provided with norms of achievement based on the performances of large numbers of pupils from more or less well defined groups. Such norms are a considerable help in score interpretation. However, such tests are not available in all, or even most, of the special fields of learning pursued in the schools. Even if a test with the proper title is available, it may turn out that the tasks it presents are not highly relevant to the objectives of instruction in a particular course. Worst of all, the easy access teachers or performance contractors have to published standardized tests opens the door to specific coaching of pupils to do well on that particular test. These problems are not insoluble. Some teachers and performance contractors have made effective use of standardized tests as external assessments of performance. In many situations, however, the disadvantages of using standardized tests will outweigh the advantages.

The alternative to using a standardized test is to build, or have built, a test designed especially to contribute data to a particular assessment problem. This approach is likely to be more costly, but to result in a test of greater relevance. The technical quality of the test may be somewhat lower. How much lower depends, in part, on how much money the user is willing to spend for its development. Finally, the possibility of harmful teaching to the test can be minimized by this approach.

The development of a custom-made test for assessment of performance should begin in a conference between teachers (or contractors) and test developers in which the objectives of instruction are stated clearly and comprehensively, a table of specifications developed, and acceptable prototype items agreed upon. Having equipped themselves with the textbooks, manuals, learning programs, and other materials used in instruction, the test developers then proceed to the writing, review, editing, and assembly of items into a test. If a remote, protected tryout and analysis of the item performance can be arranged, so much the better. If not, the scores obtained from operational use of the test ought to be analyzed to provide part of the basis for judging its adequacy.

A good custom-made test can be a very costly item. Ten thousand dollars to $20,000 is not an absurd upper limit. But, in proper hands, a reasonable facsimile of a test of highest quality can be produced for about one-tenth of those upper limits. It is not necessary that each test be designed and built with complete originality. If an existing test approximates the requirements of the new test, it can be used as at least a partial template or model for the new test.

How Can Teaching to the Test Be Prevented?

If the effectiveness of instruction is to be assessed on the basis of student performance on a test, the temptation is strong for the instructor to prepare students to handle specific questions that will be included in the test. This is often called "teaching to the test." Obviously, it is not an educationally beneficial procedure. Obviously, it tends to spoil the test as a measure of general achievement in the subject of the test. But, if the test is a readily available, published test, an insecure or short-sighted teacher is quite likely to undertake to teach to the test. Even a test specially constructed for a particular assessment task is, in effect, a "published" test once it has been used. If teachers care enough, they can find out a great deal about the particular questions included in it. So, it too may invite "teaching to the test."

Several things can be done to lessen the likelihood of teaching to the test. Teachers can be warned to avoid it and informed that their supervisors will be alert to notice it if it occurs. Pupils can be advised of its undesirability and asked to report its occurrence. Of course, the surest but most expensive way to forestall it is to prepare a new test for each new assessment effort.

Before leaving this subject, let us make an important distinction between "teaching to the test," i.e., attempting to fix in pupils' minds the answers to particular test questions, and teaching material covered by the test, i.e., attempting to give pupils the capability of answering questions like those in the test on topics covered by the test. The first is thoroughly reprehensible. The second reflects purposeful teaching. Just as there is no warrant for giving away the answers to particular questions so there is no warrant for testing pupil performance on tasks they were never taught to perform. A teacher or contractor whose work is to be assessed is entitled to know what his pupils will be expected to do. This calls for close cooperation and clear communication between teachers on the one hand and test constructors on the other. An assessment test must be thoroughly relevant to the instruction it is intended to assess. Since a test can never elicit more than a sample of performance, much more will usually be taught than can be tested. But, the test should never go beyond what has been taught.

How Should the Test
Scores Be Interpreted?

The score on an objective test usually begins as the number

of questions answered correctly. From this one can infer content meaning, e.g., what proportion of a hypothetical population of similar questions the student could also answer correctly, or roughly what fraction he knows of what he might know about a particular field of knowledge. From the number of correct answers given by each student who takes the test we can infer normative meaning, i.e., we can determine the reliability of the scores, we can estimate how accurate the scores are, that is, how likely it is that a student's actual test score differs from his hypothetical true score by 1, 2, 3, 4, or 5 score units.

These are all useful interpretations. Other interpretations, which are sometimes suggested, raise questions. For example, should a student's score after instruction be interpreted by itself or in relation to his score on a similar test before instruction? That is, should we measure gains as well as, or in place of, status?

At first glance the answer is obvious. It is the improvement brought about by instruction that should interest us, and delight or dismay us as the case may be. Unfortunately, gain scores are notoriously unreliable. If the correlation between pretest and posttest is moderately high, as it often is, most of the true score variance disappears from the difference scores. What is left are mainly errors of measurement. Stake,* basing his calculations on typical values for the reliability and standard deviation of gain scores, described what could happen in a hypothetical performance contracting situation.

Suppose that 100 students were admitted to contract instruction and pretested. After a period of time involving no training, they were tested again and the

---

*Robert E. Stake. Testing Hazards in Performance Contracting. *Phi Delta Kappan,* June 1971, 52, pp. 583-588.

students gaining a year were graduated. After another period of time, another test and another graduation. After the fourth terminal testing, even though no instruction had occurred, the chances are better than 50:50 that two-thirds of the students would have been graduated.

The unreliability of gain scores suggests that they should not be used to differentiate students who have learned more from those who have learned less. It does not mean that differences between average pretest and average posttest scores are also unsatisfactory as indicators of instructional effectiveness. The standard error of a mean of test scores is much smaller than the standard error of an individual test score. In assessing the performance of an instructional process, it is much better to use class average gains than individual pupil gains as a basis.

There is, of course, a danger in focusing attention on class average gains. It is that a teacher eager to show maximum gains might concentrate efforts on the ablest learners in the class, neglecting the slower learners. How well such a strategy would pay off is open to question. How easily a teacher could differentiate her efforts among students is also open to question. Conscientious teachers would no doubt disdain to experiment with it. If pupils are sufficiently alike in learning ability to belong in the same class, the best strategy, and the one most good teachers would be likely to follow, would seem to be to give equal attention to the instruction of each student.

Related to the question of basing assessments on gain scores is the question of taking account of pupil learning abilities in assessing educational performances. Previous achievement in learning, whether indicated by scores on achievement tests or by scores on scholastic aptitude or intelligence tests, is probably the best indication of learning abilities. This is so because previous achievements indicate the student's "track record" as a learner, and because they indicate how solid and extensive his foundation for further learning may be.

To expect a student with below average learning ability to gain as much from a particular instructional program as another student with above average learning ability is clearly unreasonable. But, while learning ability is an important determiner of success in future learning, we should guard against the notion that it is the sole determinant. For learning is an individual achievement which calls for considerable effort that only the learner himself can make. If, for any of a number of reasons, he chooses not to make the effort, or finds it unduly difficult to make, he will surely succeed badly in future learning. The important dimensions of the learner's disposition to learn and his willingness to work hard at the task are sometimes overlooked or disregarded in some of the newer instructional technologies and instructional programs.

Surely the learning abilities of the pupils do need to be taken into account in assessing the educational performances of pupils and their instructors. It is usually unwise to use a single IQ score as a sufficient measure of learning ability. It is hazardous to assess the educational performances of individual pupils in relation to their inferred learning abilities. The same kinds of errors that afflict individual gain scores, and some others, afflict estimates of individual performance in relation to ability. Achievement quotients were discredited and discarded long ago, but the same notion, involving the same errors, persists when some students are identified as underachievers and others as overachievers. But, when we assess the performance in learning of classes, in relation to the level of learning ability of the class, we are on firmer ground.

What Level of Performance Should
Be Considered Satisfactory?

When the educational performance of students is assessed to determine the amount of their learning, or to determine the effectiveness of their instructors in teaching, the results may vary from somewhere close to perfection to somewhere close to zero. The performance being assessed is a continuous variable. Often the assessments can be expressed in numbers, so that the larger of two numbers represents the greater amount of learning or the greater effectiveness of instruction. These numbers provide information that has a variety of uses, simply as descriptive information.

Sometimes, however, categorical decisions must be made. Is this amount of learning, or that degree of effectiveness of instruction satisfactory? Students may be dropped, applicants may be denied certification, teachers may be retained or dismissed on the basis of such categorical decisions. The determination of what level of performance is to be regarded as satisfactory in any particular situation is a complex and difficult problem. No simple, generally effective procedure for solving such problems will be suggested here. Probably no such procedure exists or can be developed. What can be done is to suggest certain guidelines that may facilitate discovery of an acceptable, though inevitably imperfect, solution.

One of these, obvious enough but sometimes denied, is that complete mastery in learning any but the simplest performance, or total effectiveness in instruction, is impossible. One may be the complete master of spelling a particular word, but no one ever completely masters the spelling of all English words. Perfection may be useful as an ideal goal, but we do well to recognize that it is, in fact, an unattainable goal. Those who purport to teach for mastery always are willing to settle for something less than complete mastery. Either they tolerate some degree of error or imperfection in the performances of their pupils, or they define such specific and limited goals that partial and incomplete knowledge can put on the disguise of complete mastery.

Another guideline is that completely objective, empirical determination of a minimum level of performance to be called satisfactory is out of the question. Subjective judgment and arbitrary declarations will always be involved. More of learning or skill in instruction is always better than less, but there is no point on the scale below which performances are demonstrably unsatisfactory and above which they are demonstrably satisfactory. The point is fixed by a declarative judgment. Its location is determined entirely by the values and standards of the judges who establish it.

A third guideline is that normatively based standards are likely to be more defensible than content-related standards. A standard is normatively based if it is located so that a specified proportion of the individuals in a specified group exceed or fall below it. A standard is content-related if it specifies what proportion of the tasks in a particular group of tasks must be successfully completed. Excellence and deficiency in a human performance are usually judged relative to other performances. If one can do as well as or better than the average performer, his performance is likely to be regarded as satisfactory. Most business men would not consider a 20-word per minute typist satisfactory—because it is easy to find typists who can type at three times that rate. Neither a standard which nobody meets, or which everybody meets (and some far exceed) is likely to be regarded as a satisfactory standard. Seldom is it possible to find a rational basis for setting a content-related standard.

These guidelines may be of some small help in determining a satisfactory level of performance, although they leave much of the problem to the knowledge and judgment of those who need to set standards of performance. Fortunately, the need to differentiate categorically a satisfactory from an unsatisfactory performance does not arise in most assessments of performance.

Some Recommendations

What has been said in this paper can be summarized in the following set of recommendations:

1. Recognize the fact that educational performance can be assessed, but that the process is neither simple nor easily managed.

2. Regard the performances being assessed not as ends in themselves but rather as indicators of developed competencies.

3. Accept the cultivation of cognitive competence as the main objective of schooling, with the development of affective dispositions as important by-products.

4. Define cognitive competence as acquisition of knowledge rather than as development of intellectual skills.

5. Recognize the values of objective tests in the assessment of performance.

6. Note that a fully meaningful test score carries both normative and content-related meaning.

7. Observe that the difference between a good norm-referenced test and a good criterion-referenced test is greater in theory than in practice.

8. Recognize the practical impossibility of complete mastery of any but the simplest, most specific elements of knowledge.

9. Recognize the practical impossibility of obtaining test scores which are directly proportional to the amount learned.

10. Do not expect the use of criterion-referenced tests to bring about substantial improvements in assessing educational performance.

11. Recognize the desirability or accept the inevitability of external evaluations of the effectiveness of educational programs.

12. Seek relevance in the tests used in external evaluations,

and expertness and impartiality in the testers.

13. Give preference to a custom-made test over a published standardized test for an external assessment of educational performance.

14. Guard against teaching to the test by avoiding published tests or re-use of specially constructed tests, or by warning teachers and performance contractors against it, and asking pupils and supervisors to report it.

15. Use class means rather than individual pupil scores to measure gains from instruction, or to take account of differences in learning ability.

16. Recognize the impossibility of teaching to complete mastery or of completely objective determination of a minimum satisfactory level of performance.

17. Rely more on normatively defined than on content defined standards of acceptable performance.

5.

Program Cost Analysis
in Educational Planning

SUE A. HAGGART

Any examination of alternative educational programs, including performance contracting, must be concerned with their effectiveness and cost. Because student performance is one of the measures of the effectiveness of the program, a great deal of attention is being given to the problems of setting criteria of achievement and measuring educational outcome. Less attention has been paid to the equally demanding task of estimating and analyzing the cost of educational programs. If the instructional strategies of future performance contracted programs are to be successfully utilized by educational planners, information about their cost as well as their effectiveness must be available to the decision-maker. If one is to contract for educational services, it is desirable to do so only on the basis of the best information available regarding all aspects of the proposed contract program.

This paper explores the conceptual and methodological basis of cost analysis and develops a planning cost model for estimating cost for use in evaluating alternative programs and in pre-implementation planning for future programs. The planning cost model

Sue A. Haggart is with the Resource Analysis Department of The Rand Corporation and is editor of *Program Budgeting for School District Planning*, Englewood Cliffs, New Jersey: Educational Technology Publications, 1972.

with its supporting cost analysis methodology provides a consistent basis for estimating the dollar cost of educational programs. The development of the model was undertaken because the current state of the art in costing educational programs does not provide a comparable basis for evaluating alternative programs. The usual practice is to give the cost per student for a program with no indication of what is included in the cost.

When the cost per unit of achievement is used, both the cost and the effectiveness measurement problems are severe. *Education Turnkey News* has drawn attention to several aspects of using this ratio:

> Even when accurate costs are obtained, it is difficult to compare them with school costs to see which is less, since school costs are kept and reported differently. The comparisons may reveal nothing more than different figures, especially since the firms [performance contractors in the context of this quotation] may depreciate certain items much more rapidly than schools. . . It is even more difficult to try to contrast effectiveness with cost. If effectiveness is reported in tenths of a year's achievement, which some statisticians feel is cutting it too closely, and that figure is divided into cost data which is part hidden and part hypothetical, what does the public get? Will a school board really base a major decision on curricular changes on such a "cost per unit of achievement" figure?*

The ratios of cost per student and of cost per unit of achievement

*Reed Martin and Peter Briggs. *Educational Turnkey News*, February-March 1971.

are widely used, probably because of the false confidence the "number" engenders and the relative ease with which it can be generated. In most instances, either ratio masquerades as the output of cost-effectiveness analysis. Wisely used, cost-effectiveness analysis of educational programs produces several outputs—the aspects of cost, the measures of effectiveness, and the *relationships between cost and effectiveness.* The problems and the appropriate use of cost-effectiveness analysis in educational planning have been discussed in "Cost-Effectiveness Analysis for Educational Planning."* Only very seldom is a ratio of cost per student or cost per unit achievement the appropriate end result of a cost-effectiveness analysis.

The planning cost model and its supporting methodology of educational program cost analysis provide a solid basis for resolving, at least in part, the problems encountered in determining the "cost" of educational programs. The planning cost model assists in developing comparable cost estimates of alternative programs. In this way, the model directly addresses the problems inherent in using an undefined cost per student in evaluation of different programs.

In estimating the program cost to be used in *comparing programs,* the resources available within a specific district or assets inherited from discontinued programs are *not* taken into account, and a standard price for common resources, such as teachers, is used. The resulting estimated program cost is identified as the *comparable replication cost.* It is, in essence, a comparable cost that normalizes the cost of programs.

In estimating the program cost to be used in deciding

*M.B. Carpenter and S.A. Haggart. Cost-Effectiveness Analysis for Educational Planning, *Educational Technology,* October 1970, pp. 26-30.

whether or not a particular program can be implemented in a specific district, the resources available within the district and district-specific prices for these resources must both be determined. The resulting estimated program cost in this case is the *incremental cost* to the district.

The role of the planning cost model in estimating both the comparable replication cost and the incremental cost is pictured in Figure 1. In this process, the first step, common to estimating either the comparable replication cost or the incremental cost, is a definition of the program in terms of its objectives, its students, and its resource requirements. These resource requirements are translated into the type of program cost estimate relevant to the decision to be made. The planning cost model, by providing a consistent methodology for estimating program cost, helps insure cost comparability among programs for decision-making purposes.

Before describing the planning cost model, a short discussion of the concepts and techniques of cost analysis underlying the development of the model should be helpful.

Cost Analysis

Cost analysis is concerned with the determination of physical resource requirements for the program, with calculating the program dollar cost, and with systematically evaluating the impact of changes in the program on both the resources needed and their dollar cost. The approach is to first determine the facilities, staff, equipment, materials, and services needed to conduct the educational program and then to translate these resource requirements into an estimated program cost. This sequence forces explicit consideration of the varying resource requirements for different programs or for changes in program scope.

The educational program has as its core an instructional strategy. This instructional strategy includes both the resources

Figure 1

Process of Estimating the Comparable Replication Cost
and the Incremental Cost of Programs

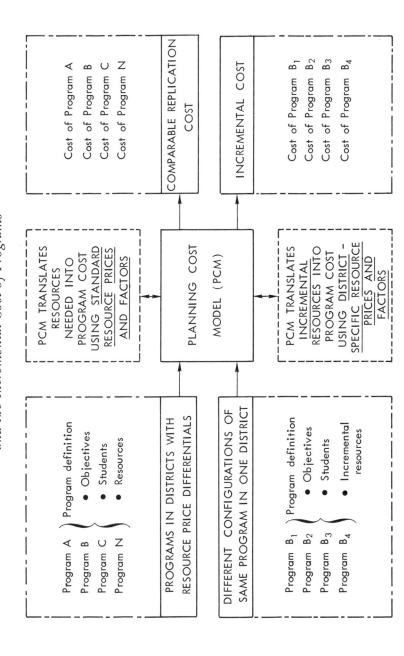

and the way in which the resources are used to produce the educational outcome.

Definition of the
Educational Program

The first step in analyzing the resource requirements and cost of a program is the definition of the program. The quality of the estimate of the cost of an educational program depends on the completeness with which the resource requirements of the program are determined. This determination, in turn, depends on the description of the educational program. The sequence of events then begins with a description of what the program is and how the program works, and continues with a determination of the quality and quantity of the resources. These resource requirements are translated into an estimate of the program dollar cost. In defining the program, the types and magnitude of support activities or services also need to be identified.

Determination of
Resource Requirements

The definition of the educational program is followed by the determination of the resource requirements. The data required are arrayed in the illustrative format of Figure 2. Some of the categories in Figure 2 pertain to resources directly. Others are "functional packages," such as training, which are combinations of resource items. Additional data should be provided as appropriate for specific programs. Each of the items in the format will be defined in terms of the kind of information needed.

Data about the characteristics of the students served and the number of students in the program will, of course, be the same data required for the evaluation of the effectiveness of the program. Data on other district conditions that might have an effect on the outcome, such as income level, turnover rate, or mobility, should be provided. The instructional time should be given, along with other information that relates to determining the actual time spent with subgroups of students or individual students. The student/teacher ratio is usually used as a proxy for this, but an effort should be made to refine this piece of information.

Figure 2

*Format for Program and
Resource Information*

Characteristics of Students Served

Number of Students

Instructional Data
  Class time
  Class size

Facilities
  Space
  Students/classroom/day
  Utilization
  Furnishings

Staffing
  Teachers
  Special teachers
  Paraprofessionals
  Other personnel

Equipment
  Program-related
  Student-related

Materials
  Program-related
  Student-related

Pre-service Training

In-service Training

Other Support

In describing the facilities needed, the space requirements, including mobile or portable classrooms, laboratories, and their utilization rates, should be carefully determined. The requirements for non-school facilities should also be stated. The special needs for electrical outlets, air conditioning, carpeting, and lighting should be identified. Furniture needs are to be specified, identifying any special per-student requirements.

Staffing for the program should be described in terms of the qualifications needed as well as in terms of number (e.g., give number of certificated or certified teachers, the number of special teachers, paraprofessional staff, and other personnel involved in the program). If a staff member works less than full time, the percent of the time involved should be given. Staff requirements for time beyond the "normal" school day should be stated. This includes, for example, custodial or security services needed to keep the school open after the regular day.

Equipment and materials should be identified as program-related, classroom-related, or student-related. Program-related equipment or material is that which will be used by several students during the day or some time period of the program. Very often the equipment or materials may be grouped by classroom unit. Student-related equipment or material is that which is required because there is a specific number of students in the program. An additional distinction should be made about the consumable nature of the materials and about the lifetime of the equipment. The same treatment should be applied to supplies if the usual district practice is to treat equipment and supplies as separate categories.

The amount of time involved in pre-service and in-service training should be specified. The materials or equipment required should be given. It should be noted if the training time is included as part of the regular time of the staff or if it is incremental to the regular working hours. If in-service training time is a substantial part of the individual teacher's time, additional teachers (or substitute teachers) may be required for the instructional load of the program.

The requirement for program-related services such as evaluation or other management activities should be given. It is preferable if the actual time or the numbers of consultants can be specified. In either case, the purpose is to provide some estimate of the magnitude of these services so that the decision can be made on what it costs to buy the service rather than to develop, if possible, an in-house capability.

Support from other activities means the support required by the educational program from such service programs as bus transportation. For example, a particular educational program might need bus transportation for field trips. This instructionally required transportation is over and above the cost of home-to-school transportation.

The resource requirements identified in Figure 2 are meant to be suggestive only. If other data are available, they should be given, since the purpose is to define as completely as possible those resources and cost-generating activities needed to carry out the educational program.

The resource requirements are then translated into the dollar estimates of program cost—either the comparable replication cost or the incremental cost. A planning cost model provides a framework for systematically and consistently estimating program cost.

The Planning Cost Model

The planning cost model provides the mechanism to determine, conveniently and consistently, the cost of various alternative programs. By design, the model is appropriate for pencil-and-paper operation as well as computer operation.*

The model provides the framework for bringing together the resources (facilities, staff, equipment, materials) required to carry out an educational program and for relating these resources to program output in the form of activities.

By relating the inputs required to produce outputs, in terms of activities, the model provides more information for making decisions about the merit of selected changes in the activity structure of the total program. For example, trade-offs between fewer but longer instructional periods and more but shorter periods could be assessed. The model also provides the basis for examining the cost consequences, for the total program, of changes in the resource utilization rate (i.e., student/teacher ratio) or in resource cost (i.e., teacher salary).

The task of constructing the model demanded a close examination of the concepts of cost analysis, especially in their application to educational program cost methodology. This examination resulted in the delineation of an approach to costing educational programs. Basic to this is the definition of a preliminary list of cost categories. Those costs of school district operation *not* affected by the existence of the program are not included in the estimated cost of the program. An example will serve to clarify this point.

The district cost category, transportation, provides for the transportation of students to and from school. Students in the special program will continue to receive transportation, if they need it, just as though they were not in the special program but were, instead, students in the regular program. This regular transporta-

*A planning cost model designed for computer operation is described in R-672-SJS, *Project R-3, San Jose, California: Evaluation of Results and Development of a Cost Model,* M.L. Rapp, M.B. Carpenter, S.A. Haggart, S.H. Landa, and G.C. Sumner, The Rand Corporation, March 1971.

tion cost is not included in the cost of the individual program. But, if the instructional method of the special program calls for field trips or other activities requiring transportation, the cost of this transportation is included as a cost of the special program.

Cost Categories

The items, services, people, and activities and their cost required for an educational program can be brought together in one format—the cost element structure shown in Figure 3. These cost elements are grouped into two broad categories: the acquisition cost and the operational cost. The cost of most programs can be adequately encompassed within these two broad categories. The acquisition cost is the one-time cost to acquire a capability. The operational cost is the continuing cost to maintain a capability over a period of time. In the following discussion, one year's operating cost is assumed.

The acquisition, or one-time, cost to acquire a capability is, in practice, also referred to as initial, investment, or capital cost. It covers the cost of all resources required to acquire a capability. The cost of the effort devoted to research, development, or design of components of the program or alternatives should be included as part of this cost. The cost of designing a different mathematics curriculum, for example, is a development cost. In estimating the *comparable replication* cost, however, some overall development costs might be treated as sunk costs. That is, the first program to use the new curriculum would incur this expense, and subsequent programs using the curriculum would inherit the new curriculum on a cost-free basis. On the other hand, if the curriculum had to be redesigned for a particular program, this would be a development cost for that program.

The operational cost is also referred to as the recurring or continuing cost to maintain the capability. The cost of modifica-

Figure 3

Cost Element Structure for
Educational Programs

Acquisition Cost

Design of program*
Development of materials*
Evaluation design*
Program implementation
Equipment
  Program-related
  Student-related
Materials and supplies
  Program-related
  Student-related
Pre-service training
Facilities (space)
Installation

Operational Cost

Program direction*
Evaluation*
Management support*
Salaries
  Teachers
  Paraprofessionals
  Specialists
  Other
In-Service training
Materials and supplies
  Program-related
  Student-related
Equipment
  Replacement
  Maintenance
Facilities O & M
Contracted services
Media services
Transportation

*In an operational program, as opposed to a demonstration program, there might be no program cost associated with these activities.

tion of facilities and the cost of in-service training of teachers are included as an operational cost to maintain the program. These broad categories of cost—acquisition and operation—are used as a basis for organizing the cost elements into the cost element structure.

This structure provides the framework for identifying the cost of the program in an operational environment. Each element, whether it is an item purchased or an estimate of activity cost, will be discussed. But first, remember that costs not varying because of the existence of the program are not included. For example, district-wide administrative costs are not allocated.

Costs that might be incurred in a demonstration program but not in an *operational* program are identified by an asterisk in Figure 3. Some of the cost categories can be characterized as the cost of activities rather than the cost of items purchased. In many instances, the items purchased quite clearly underlie the cost of activities, but the activity cost, however, may be used directly in estimating the program cost. For example, the evaluation cost of a program might be estimated by using a factor such as cost per student. Or, the cost per program might be used if the evaluation is done by an outside contractor or evaluator. If appropriate, these would be the factors used to estimate the *operational* cost of evaluation. The *acquisition* cost—the non-recurring cost—for evaluation might be based on the district staff time to design the evaluation of the program or might simply be the cost charged by the outside evaluator. The cost basis for these inputs would be per *program* for acquisition cost and per *student* or *program* for the operational cost.

Cost Basis for Inputs

The cost basis for all inputs for the categories in the cost element structure is shown in Table 1. For each category the cost basis is either per student, per program, per unit, or direct service charge. The per student and per program distinction is rather obvious; the per unit basis refers to units such as classrooms, resource centers, and language laboratories. The service basis is used when the input to the model might be the extent of a service performed either within the district or by an outside source. An example of the former would be the operation and maintenance of

Table 1

The Cost Basis for Inputs

Categories	COST BASIS Student	Program	Unit	Service
Acquisition Cost				
Design of program		X		
Development of materials		X		
Evaluation design		X		
Program implementation		X		
Equipment				
Program-related		X	X	
Student-related	X			
Materials				
Program-related		X	X	
Student-related	X			
Pre-service training		X		X
Facilities	X			
Installation			X	
Operational Cost				
Program direction		X		
Evaluation	X	X		
Management support		X		
Salaries				
Teachers	X			
Paraprofessionals	X			
Specialists	X	X		
Other	X	X		
In-Service training		X		X
Materials and supplies				
Program-related		X	X	
Student-related	X			
Equipment				
Replacement			X	
Maintenance			X	
Facilities O & M				X
Contracted services	X			X
Media services	X			X
Transportation	X			X

the facilities; the latter service-based input might cover such items as the contracted transportation for the instructional part of a program or the provision of so many hours of instructional television.

In some cases, the cost input basis might be a combination of program and unit (classroom), of student and service, or of program and service. No rigidity is implied. The intent is to provide an understanding of how the inputs of the model are categorized. This categorization is basic to the structure of the planning cost model. At this time, it is only necessary to emphasize that some level of input is required because there is a certain number of students, and other levels of input are required because there is a certain number of classrooms or instructional centers. In many cases, there is a *program* cost that is independent of the number of students or centers.

Outputs and Inputs
of the Model

A program-related cost can be a throughput to the model. For example, the cost of program development would be both an input and output. The cost of pre-service training for the teachers in the program is calculated within the model. The physical descriptors of the program and cost factors, such as the number of teachers, the salary cost, the cost per mile, are the inputs to the model. The objective is to keep the number of inputs to a workable minimum while allowing enough input flexibility to provide useful outputs of the model for the evaluation and planning of educational programs.

The outputs of the model are, in general, the resource and cost information about the specific educational program. The *descriptors of the program*—number of teachers; number of students; space requirements; equipment, materials, and supplies;

and need for services such as transportation or evaluation—are *shown right along with the cost output*. The purpose is to provide, in one place, an estimate of the comparable replication cost and a description of what is being bought. As this practice becomes more prevalent, the use of a cost per student to describe an unknown quantity will decrease and the quality of information available to the educational planner will increase.

The output of the model is illustrated in Figures 4 and 5. Notice the similarity of the format to the cost element structure of Figure 3. More detailed information for any of the items shown can be provided in supporting reports. For example, the resources and cost underlying the cost per student hour under Media Services might be of interest for some types of decisions. The supporting detail for this would follow the same cost element structure used for estimating the cost of the entire educational program.

The inputs of the model fall into three broad groups: (1) the physical descriptors of the program; (2) the cost of resources and services; and (3) the factors or estimating relationships. The physical descriptors, including the type and quantity of resources, were shown in Figure 2, *Format for Program and Resource Information*. In short, these inputs describe the students, the educational program, and the resource requirements. Inputs are required for all the changes, or variables, that make one program different from another program.

The inputs describe the cost of resources and services and cover such items as the cost of equipment used, the salaries of the staff, the cost of testing, the cost of transportation, and the cost of training. The input factors, or estimating relationships, include both cost factors such as cost of materials per student and non-cost estimating relationships such as number of in-service training days per teacher.

The Structure of the Model

The model integrates the program description, in terms of resources required, with the process of estimating the program cost. This process begins with the determination of resource requirements and continues with the translation of these resource requirements into an estimate of dollar cost. Both the acquisition

Figure 4

Summary Output of the Model

Description of Program

Program:	Objective:
Staffing:	Student Characteristics:
Facilities:	
Equipment:	Operational Characteristics:
	Instructional time
Materials:	Student grouping
	Location

Acquisition Cost

Program activities	$ xxx
Equipment	xx
Facilities	xx
Materials	xx
Total acquisition cost..$ xxxx	

Operational Cost

Program activities	$ xxx
Salaries	xxxx
Materials	xx
Supplies	xx
Equipment	xx
Other support	xx
Total operational cost..$xxxxx	

Figure 5

Detailed Output of Program Cost Estimate

Acquisition Cost

Program Activities:	Design of Program	$ xxx	
	Development of Materials	xxx	
	Evaluation Design	xxx	
	Program Implementation	xxxx	
	Pre-service Training	xxx	
	Installation	xxx	
			$xxxxx
Equipment:	Program-related	$ xxx	
	Student-related	xxx	
			xxxx
Facilities:	Student-related	$ xxx	
			xxx
Materials:	Program-related	$ xx	
	Student-related	xx	
			xxx
	Total Acquisition Cost		$xxxxx

Operational Cost

Program Activities:	Program Direction	$ xxx	
	Evaluation	xxx	
	Management Support	xx	
	In-service Training	xx	
	Facilities O & M	xx	
	Contracted Services	xx	
	Media Services	xx	
	Transportation	xx	
			$ xxxx
Salaries:	Teachers	xxxx	
	Specialists	xxx	
	Paraprofessionals	xxx	
	Other	xxx	
			xxxx
Materials:	Program-related	xx	
	Student-related	xx	
			xxx
Supplies:	Program-related	xx	
	Student-related	xx	
			xx
Equipment:	Replacement	xx	
	Maintenance	xx	
			xx
Other Support:			xx
	Total Operational Cost		$xxxxx

cost and the operational cost are estimated. The model's framework for estimating the acquisition and the operational cost is shown in Figures 6 and 7, respectively. For each cost category, there is an estimate of cost on either a student, program, unit, or service basis. In the case of "units," the estimate can be the cost per teacher, the cost of the equipment per classroom or instructional center, or the cost per student or materials consumed. For some cost categories, the estimate can be based on an overall program cost. For example, the pre-service training, if done by an outside contractor, might be a total cost for the program. It could also be a cost per teacher.

In the cost category for Materials, the cost estimate may require an estimate for the cost for student-related materials, for the cost of materials in the classroom for use by many students, and for the cost of materials used by the staff in conducting the program. The same practice is followed for the cost categories of the framework for the operational cost in Figure 7.

The cost categories provide a convenient way to identify the data needed about the educational program and its operation in order to estimate its cost. The data for the cost categories for both the acquisition and operational cost are shown separately in Figures 8 and 9, respectively.

Program cost analysis provides the information needed by the district in making decisions about whether to plan the implementation of a program, and, if so, what configuration of program can be afforded within the resource constraints of the district. As a final note, two points should be made clear. First, these cost estimates are *planning* cost estimates. Much greater detail and accuracy are required to meet the needs of actual implementation and financial accountability. Second, analysis of the dollar-cost alone does not provide adequate information for educational decisions; for this reason, the emphasis here is on the analysis of both the dollar and non-dollar resources for alternative programs.

Figure 6

The Planning Cost Model: Acquisition Cost

Cost Category	Student	Program	Unit	Services
Design of Program		$/Program		
Development of Materials		$/Program		
Evaluation Design		$/Program		$/Service
Program Implementation		$/Program		
Pre-service Training		$/Program	$/Teacher	$/Service
Installation		$/Program	$/Equipment	
Equipment	$/Student	$/Program	$/Classroom $/Resource Center	
Facilities	$/Student		$/Resource Center	
Materials	$/Student	$/Program	$/Classroom	
Other Support	$/Student	$/Program	$/Classroom	$/Service

Figure 7

The Planning Cost Model: Operational Cost

Cost Category	Student	Program	Unit	Services
Program Direction		$/Program		
Evaluation		$/Program		$/Service
Management Support		$/Program		$/Service
Facilities O & M			$/Space	
Contracted Services				$/Service
Media Services				$/Service
Transportation	$/Student	$/Program		
Salaries (including fringe benefits)				
Teachers			$/Teacher	
Specialists			$/Specialist	
Paraprofessionals			$/Aide	
Other			$/Type	
Materials				
Program-related	$/Student	$/Program		
Student-related	$/Student			
Supplies				
Program-related		$/Program		
Student-related	$/Student			
Equipment				
Replacement			$/Unit	
Maintenance			$/Unit	
Other Support	$/Student	$/Program	$/Unit	$/Service

Figure 8

Program Data: Acquisition Cost Categories

Cost Category	Data Requirements
Design of Program Development of Material Evaluation Design Program Implementation Pre-Service Training Installation	• If these activities are required for the program, the *number*, the *type* of personnel involved, the *time* spent, and salary are needed.
Equipment	• The equipment list is determined for each student, for each classroom, and, if applicable, for the program. The classroom's equipment is used by several classes of students. The number of students that can use the equipment is specified.
Facilities	• The space required is that over and above the regular program; both for each student or for special resource centers.
Materials	• The initial stock of materials is determined for each student, for each classroom, and, if applicable, for the program.

Figure 9

Program Data: Operational Cost Categories

Cost Category	Data Requirements
Program Direction Evaluation Management Support	• The number and type of staff, the time spent for each activity, and salary are needed for this.
Salaries (with fringe benefits)	• All instructional staff and direct support classes of staff are identified by broad category; i.e., general teachers, specialists, and aides rather than a teacher with a specific salary are used. Fringe benefits are included at the district percentage factor.
Materials and Supplies	• The type and quantity of materials used are specified on a student and program basis.
Equipment	• The equipment maintenance factor and the equipment replacement factor (based on the estimated lifetime of the equipment) are applied to the equipment used in the program.
Facilities O & M Contracted Services Media Services Transportation	• The program requirements for each of the categories are specified in terms of square feet maintained, services purchased, number of hours of audio-visual instruction and bus trip mileage.

6.

Performance Toward What Result?
An Examination of Some Problems
in Outcome Measurement

SELMA J. MUSHKIN

Up to a very short time ago, a single criterion—achievement of skills, such as reading—was applied in judging success or failure (or its score value) of an education program. The issue of a multi-dimensional educational product was a subject of much debate; it was debated whether attitudes and attributes were at all useful in assessing product, let alone necessary. Among the influences at work was the simplistic drive to get at "real measurements" of cost-effectiveness in place of vague generalities about goals. Despite the merit of the undertaking, some basic concepts of effectiveness measurement were set aside in the drive to show analytical studies would provide useful policy tools—and to *count* program effectiveness. Discussions in 1966 with OEO officials and with those in the Office of Education made plain this insistence that achievement test scores, and those alone, served as sufficient measurements. Whatever else education might produce, was the argument, it surely must produce basic skills, such as reading, and if other products were of any importance, perhaps alternative programs or activities could achieve them better. To counterbalance this emphasis on achievement measurement was to

Selma J. Mushkin is Professor of Economics and Director of the Public Services Laboratory at Georgetown University.

question the whole exercise—to question the value of hard analysis.

Nowadays, in the course of analysis of educational programs and their evaluation, dimensions other than achievement scores are in the ascent, and it seems unlikely that present trends will be reversed. Partly this is a consequence of the findings of the evaluation studies themselves; partly it is a result of more interdisciplinary effort in which the skills of philosophy, sociology, psychology, and anthropology are being brought to bear on educational outcomes along with the tools of the economist. In the last six years or so, educational research has shown consistently that various characteristics of the children's home environment, particularly parental attitudes, strongly influence children's achievement.[1/2] Parental aspirations for the child have been found to be better predictors of school attainment than variables related to the school itself. At the same time, research on the development of intelligence and achievement has indicated the gains that come about from experience, especially social experiences, are essential ingredients in the developmental process.[3/4] Teacher expectation as part of that social experience has been shown to influence learning.

Basic criteria of effectiveness for evaluation purposes call for a series of properties in the criteria used. These include (1) relevance to the objectives being measured; (2) completeness in encompassing the whole of the objectives formulated; and (3) measurability.

While use of insufficient measurements or measurements that match inadequately the full range and meaning of the objectives formulated required caution in acceptance of results of evaluation studies based on achievement scores alone, the persistence of negative findings has had marked policy impact. On the basis of a review of studies, one American expert suggested "the difficulty seems to be that it is becoming clear that factors that can be varied with money are not very closely related to the achievement of school pupils."[5]

Feedback effects of education evaluation studies are reflected in the President's April, 1970 Message to the Congress: "We will ask the Congress to supply many more dollars for education . . . but only if we get more education for the dollar." The President led the nation in saying that the most pressing need of the schools is not for more money, but for reform. The questioning of state aid for schools and the enlarged opposition to property tax increases for schools follow from the repetitive negative evaluation study findings on achievement scores.

Emphasis on achievement scores has had an impact on processes of education as well. If the achieving of skills or proficiency in such matters as reading is, in fact, the purpose of the school, it is but a small step to:

- The undertaking to teach to the specified skills that are required. (When the skills sought are rigorously identified and specified, and measures of those skills are designed and implemented, teaching programs can be directed. If the skills learned are deficient, a special program can be designed, e.g., Right to Read program.)
- The review of incentives for the teaching of those specified skills. (If the skills are known and also the methods of teaching, then presumably the implementation of the method can be encouraged by incentives.)
- The design of new incentives for performance of teacher and student. (When processes for encouraging teaching and learning are not readily at hand, then additional research on incentives should prove useful.)
- New experimentation with teaching methods when processes are not known.

Performance contracting has its origin in this emphasis on achievement scores. It provides both a means to stimulate learning and teaching of the specific skills, and also a base for new experimentation with processes of teaching and learning.

In the current scene, performance of education toward educational results has major importance. The difficulties of defining results sought, or outcomes, and of assessing by measurements those results and outcomes, are many. Among the steps required are these:

1. To define outcome appropriately in terms of purpose, and if necessary, to define outcome multidimensionally.
2. To explore what is known about measurement of the defined outcomes.
3. To examine the state of the art on instrumentation to improve the measurements.
4. To assess interaction of the defined outcomes.
5. To select proxy measurements for use.
6. To test and retest through use the outcome proxies selected.
7. To identify from among the testing instruments those that could be applied as proxies.

Steps taken to define outcome measurements and to implement such measurements carry additional responsibilities, for the feedback effects are many and can hardly be ignored. Among the feedback effects are these:

*   Concentration on the "proxy" rather than the underlying learning sought.
*   Direction of funds to improve the "proxy," for example, the reading readiness program.
*   Possible changes in the learning of children.

If reading skills of children are rewarded, then reading scores tend to be emphasized, both in teaching and resource allocation. A numbers game is generated on the proxy. Proxies intended as simplifiers become popularizers; or, stated differently, the focus is on the proxy measure and data collected about it. There are other feedback effects as well. The proxy measurements, as is indicated later, can affect the child himself and his learning. Among the additional steps that need to be taken are these:

1. To assemble what is known about the impact of measurable factors on learning.
2. To study feedback effects on learning of criteria for judging learning.
3. To study feedback effects on policy of criteria for learning.
4. To determine what is known about how to create each of the identified outcomes.

In the present paper I have tried to consider some of the problems of measurements, viewing measurements from the perspective of performance as consumption (both in the immediate period and in the longer run), and also as an investment. The research on which this paper draws was done for the National Center for Educational Statistics in a small scale exploratory study of statistical measurements of educational outcomes. In that small initial project, only a beginning could be made on the many problems involved in outcome measurement. By and large the emphasis has been on a taxonomy of outcome measurements and review of data sources and instrumentation that could be applied in a statistical gathering effort. Thus, "pad and pencil" tests are those given primary attention.

Outcomes of education appear to be four-dimensional, if an

economist may be forgiven for intruding a description dealing with economic immeasurables. A review of some of the work that has been done on education outcomes in other disciplines suggests that these outcomes may be classified as the four A's: (1) attributes; (2) aptitudes; (3) attitudes; and (4) achievements. Together the proxies chosen for these four A's would enable the exploration of a number of multi-sectoral aspects of education and perhaps provide a better understanding of the dynamics of educational outcomes. With the four general sets of criteria, it would appear possible to probe much more deeply into the results of education and to ascertain whether earlier evaluation studies are wide of the mark or, in fact, are sufficient.

Complexities are even greater, for education has both short-run products and long-term ones. What product definition captures each of the phases in a continuum that creates the "being" of boy, and then man? Characteristically education in economic terms may be regarded both as an investment and as a consumer good. Outcome definitions associated with each of those purposes are very different and the consequences of the measures for policy differ, too. The "investment" may be tested in terms of rates of return, or by changes in employment, occupations, and earnings. As a consumer good, education is perhaps described more vaguely as to quality and quantity of product. Education as a consumer good gives "well-being," "joy," "happiness." In one aspect, the consumer good is "durable"; in others, enjoyment may be momentary. In common with other market goods, it may be tested by consumer decisions taken. Votes on school bond issues provide a measure, but even such decisions are subject to much ambiguity and, not unimportantly, even the decision about who is the consumer is not clear—the child or his parent? Public school systems, operating as they do, as monopolies, mean consumer choices are narrowed greatly. Voting behavior rather than market behavior records the public choice.

Short-Run and
Consumer Measurements

Essentially, product definition in education concerns itself with changes in behavior that come about through changes in attitudes, ferreting out and development of aptitudes and attributes, and the achievement of skills. Outcome measurements can hardly ignore behavior change so central to the objectives of educational services.

Achievement and aptitude (or ability) testing as "product" indexes have received much of the attention in the past among the "soft" social sciences; economists only recently directed their attention to short-run results. Jerome Bruner summed up the concern with measuring achievements in this way: Schools do not look to the creation of self-confident fools.[6]

Aptitude. Aptitude measurements are perhaps the earliest of the measurement undertakings and the most widely applied. Aptitude (defined here to be synonomous with ability) is not to be regarded, the social sciences' findings show, as an inherited "static" characteristic. Ability indexes have been used by economists as if they were independent of "education"; this use is not warranted by the research.[7] Certainly ability as measured does not constitute a valid "correction" of school outputs to be introduced into production function or economic growth analysis. Part of the outcome in performance contracting, as in other educational processes, is to discover and develop talents and to raise aptitude (ability) levels.

Achievements. Following on the work of Alfred Binet and Theodore Simon, the idea of scale was applied not only to intelligence but to achievement testing as well. Thorndike and his students, for example, developed scales for measuring achievement in arithmetic (1908), handwriting (1910), spelling (1913), drawing (1913), reading (1914), and language ability (1916). Other

universities, particularly Chicago, joined Columbia in its efforts.[8]
And by 1918 the National Society for the Study of Education
published its yearbook on *The Measurement of Educational
Products.*

Thorndike's work in 1918 sounds much the same as the
vocabulary of educational program analysts today. "Education is
concerned with changes in human beings; a change is a difference
between two conditions; each of these conditions is known to us
mainly by the products produced by it—things made, words
spoken, acts performed, and the like. To measure any of these
products means to define its amount in some way so that
competent persons will know how large it is, better than they
would without measurement."[9]

Measurement work on achievement and ability has continued
at an accelerating pace, spurred on in the immediate period by the
more widespread support for evaluation of educational programs.
The Mental Measurements Yearbook was published in 1937; by
the sixth yearbook, published in 1965, 1,219 tests were included.
Their distribution by classification suggests that about 15 percent
of the tests related to personality, a little over 11 percent to
intelligence, and the remainder to achievements in such skills as
English, mathematics, foreign languages.

Drawing on the information provided in surveys of state
testing—surveys made by the Educational Testing Service in 1967,
the Akron Public School Survey (April, 1968) of basic testing
programs used in major school systems, are the 1969 Survey of
Compensatory Education—it was found that some five or six tests
accounted for a large fraction of all the tests given. The tests
widely used are these: Iowa Tests of Educational Development,
Stanford Achievement Tests, Sequential Tests of Education
Progress, California Achievement Tests, Iowa Tests of Basic Skills,
Metropolitan Achievement Tests, and SRA Achievement Series.

For most tests given, national norms and regional norms have been developed by test publishers; and in those states in which state testing has been done for some period—New York, Alabama, California, Rhode Island, Minnesota, Pennsylvania—statewide norms are available.

Measurements using achievement tests as a proxy for the product "learning" are at best partial, and portion out, by "average group performance," learning into grade levels.[10] "There is no wide agreement on specific subject matter for each grade. There has been a great shift in what is considered proper learning for given ages and grades in some subjects, and it appears that even greater changes are in the offing."[11]

Despite concerns about the meaning of a grade level standard, scores according to grade levels, particularly in reading, are widely applied. "Grade equivalent" simply means median performance in the norming sample at a given grade at the time of test standardization. The norming of the test and the representativeness of those norms clearly affect what is counted as grade level.

Roger Lennon's discussion of norms in a 1963 ETS paper notes:

> There are good reasons for supposing that differences in norms ascribable simply to . . . variations in norming procedures are not negligible. When we consider that to such differences from test to test there must be added differences associated with varying content, and with the time at which standardization programs are conducted (including the time of the school year), the issue of comparability, or lack of it, among the results of the various tests may begin to be seen in proper perspective. Empirical data reveal that there may be variations of as much as a year and a half in grade equivalent among the

results yielded by various achievement tests; variations
of as much as 8 to 10 points of IQ among various
intelligence tests are, of course, by no means un-
common.[12]

The development of score correspondence from reading test
to reading test is essential to any nationwide data collection effort
that leaves to the local community and state the initial decision on
what children should learn and are learning.

In that context, a feasibility survey was launched in 1969 on
reading comprehension subtests for the most widely used standardized test batteries, appropriate for children in grades four, five,
and six. The reading comprehension subtests of the five most
widely used test batteries were administered to over 830 children,
with each child completing subtests from three batteries, arranged
in a random order. From the test results, computation was made
of correlation coefficients among the five tests with the finding of
a high correlation among tests. The correlation coefficient for
groups of grade four pupils that was lowest was 0.81 and the
highest correlation for this grade was 0.91.

Based on the results of this feasibility survey, a major test
equating and standardization study is now underway. Among the
purposes are these:

- to set up nationally representative norms for reading
  comprehension and vocabulary subtests;
- to develop tables of score correspondence between
  subtests of the Metropolitan and corresponding subtests
  of levels of six other test batteries based on a new
  representative sample of population of children enrolled
  in grades four, five, and six in both public and
  nonpublic schools;

- to correlate correspondence of the several test batteries based on the newly collected scores from a sample of the appropriate national populations; and
- to prepare tables of score correspondence for samples of several national subpopulations.

Attributes and Attitudes. While achievement scores received early use in program evaluation, attributes and attitudes are increasingly emphasized as part of educational outcomes. The President in his April, 1970 Message to the Congress regarding education emphasized such characteristics as "humanity," "wit," and "responsibility," and more recently the Secretary of Health, Education, and Welfare, in emphasizing consumption ends of education, called attention to the importance of "self-confidence," "curiosity," and "love of learning."[13] Among the numerous measurements, some attributes receive the major attention, particularly "perception of self" and some attitudes such as "perception of society" in relation to self. Many words clearly are used in describing the attitudes and attributes, but what is being identified on the one hand is the dignity of "being," the child as child into adulthood, and on the other is the attitudes toward society that make for motivation toward betterment.

Numerous measurements and the scales on attributes and attitudes are available. The range of the studies carried out are suggested by the chapter headings and chapter contents in two handbooks of measurements[14/15]—one on sociological measurements and the other on measurements of political attitudes.

The Social Sciences Research Center has compiled measurements to assess their usefulness and to work toward definitional standardization as well as more widespread implementation of tested instruments. The American Psychological Association additionally has made technical recommendations on psychological testing and diagnostic methods.[16] Considerable progress has been made toward uniformity and standardization of testing by development of the Minnesota Multi-Phasic Personality Inventory. In addition, Guilford and Zimmerman[17] and also Cattell have attempted to standardize concepts with respect to personality. To illustrate, a handbook[18] for the 16 personality factor question-naire prepared by Cattell and Eber contains profiles describing personality test scores of large samples in over 40 occupations. Evaluation techniques as they are applied in program analysis, moreover, have begun to be applied to mental health programming and to patient care in such a way as to encourage uniform design of criteria and uniform testing for evaluation purposes. (The program evaluation project of Hennepin County, Minnesota, is a major example.)[19]

In research on educational outcomes at the Public Services Laboratory of Georgetown University, self-esteem as an attribute, and external-internal control as an attitude have been identified as having major power in determining achievement.

**Output: Sequence of Performance and
Longer-Run Product**

Education as a sequential and continuing process points to parallel sequences in outcomes measurements. The multiproducts have somewhat different time dimensions.

The duality of purposes of education, or rather the possi-bility of considering the objectives of education (and measures of results) at different points in time, is illustrated by Table 1.

If educational achievement is heavily dependent on attitudes and attributes, as studies seem to show, the time periods within which attitudes and attributes can be altered are extremely important for understanding performance contracting and its timing problems. One year's gain in achievement for one year's

Table 1

Summary Classification of Outputs

	Time 1			Time 2		Time 3
	Product consumption		Investment	Investment feedbacks		Inter-generational impacts
	Quantity	Quality	Income		Consumption feedback	
STUDENTS	e.g., high school completion	4 A's	Employment	Economic growth		Educational motivation
			e.g., school dropouts,		e.g., medical care uses	
			e.g., value added		e.g., consumer efficiency	
					e.g., use of leisure time	
					e.g., moral and citizenship values	
PARENTS	Babysitting					
	Votes on bonds, etc.					

input essentially neglects the difficulties of altering a child's attitudes and attributes.

Follow-up Measurements.   Single-period performance accounting does not adequately reflect child behavior. If many among those children tested happen to be on a temporary plateau in learning, the results of measured achievement may not fully reflect the preparatory absorption of knowledge that is on-going. Important questions are being raised about sequence and learning.

Presumably, testing designs must follow curriculum phasing step by step, phase by phase, just as curriculum must parcel out information to be learned. Scoring of information acquired has to be defined and examined in small parcels. Programmed instruction is an extreme of this detailing and specification of what is judged to be the learning requirement, with testing made a part of the learning experience itself. For performance measurement, standardized tests may not always be regarded as appropriate. In any case, residual concerns about national uniformity in testing will persist in sufficient force so that the result is multiple testing instruments, and, perhaps for some time, continuing reliance on private agency rather than public testing, or more statewide involvement in achievement testing.[20]

In terms of both performance contracting and statistical measurements, the sequential facets of education suggest follow-through studies—performance not for single years but periods of time.[21] Rivlin has urged that a longitudinal data system be developed to keep track of individual children and their family background as they move through school, and for recording changes in their performance.[22] She also has urged detailed program information at the level of the individual child to reveal, for example, not just whether he was in a school that had a remedial reading program but how many hours he spent in the program and the kind of program it was. Longitudinal studies are now being planned by the U.S. Office of Education to gather data on, among other things, educational outcomes. Studies underway or planned call for data collection on high school graduates and also for first grade children. Much information is being sought about the child, including his prenatal care, grades, and achievement scores. The intent of the early childhood schedule is to follow children through grade levels 3, 6, and 8, as well as the first grade period.

Preparatory vs. the present. The length of the schooling period (one sixth to one quarter of a lifetime) itself argues against exclusive concern with *preparatory* education. The investment or opportunity costs come to a substantial share of total living time. As a consequence of focusing on the child and his moment of living in determining the product named "education," much more weight comes to be placed on pleasurability, on feeling good, on being, and on joyful doing. (By and large, I am tending to use non-specific psychological or sociological terms to make plain that I have no expertise in their use.)

Changing circumstances together with the advances in the processes of research in educational outcomes has led to a rediscovery of the consumption purposes of education.

For one thing, the payoff for educational investment appears to be falling off. Differential years in school are diminishing as the nominal average or median years of schooling is responding to automatic in-school promotions and the pressures against dropping out of school, and fewer and fewer persons remaining in the work force have only eight years of schooling. A number of studies, such as that of Samuel Bowles, of earnings differentials associated with skill differences[2,3] show very large relative changes in skill content have been accompanied by very small earning differences. For a substantial period of years, despite the marked improvement in numbers of years of schooling, relative wages of college graduates or high school graduates (and the later wages) or to those of 8th graders remained fairly constant. More recently, when general demand has not been sufficient to maintain high employment, the stability of earnings differentials is weakening, perhaps giving weight to the thesis of Ivar Berg's *The Great Training Robbery*[24] in which he attacks the productivity or rate of return from schooling, arguing essentially that education is providing formal credentials of "progressively less economic importance."

Mary Jean Bowman is one of the scholars who has moved the discussion further by changing the concept of output from a skill learned to the outcome in interest in learning that skill.

> Only when we view men as men, not as bundles of skills, can we understand the role of education in economic growth or the effects of growth on incentives to undertake further education. Education becomes a means to enhance ability to learn and to adapt.

> Although there have been voices urging that the important contribution of education in production was specifically what it did to a man's ability to learn and to adapt in dynamic situations, little attention has been paid to this proposition in the canonical rate-of-return literature.[25]

In the course of scientific inquiry of economic phenomena, a deeper penetration of educational outcomes has been made.

If differences in skill levels acquired do not explain earnings variations, what does? Is it work motivation; or, to use a Veblenian term, "the instinct of workmanship"? Kelvin Lancaster, for example, has pushed the economist's view of consumption to examining the basic characteristics of the product relevant to the consumer.[26]

Traditionally, education policies have considered substantive education as preparatory for later living. Only with the formulation of the idea of human capital and investment in people were financial and program policies of education redesigned so that they might be more compatible with the concept of education as preparatory.

Economists began to apply the tools of their discipline and the concomitant measurements to education in the early 1960s. And in this application, the quantitative measurement of outcome for policy strategies essentially has its roots. Theodore Schultz initiated work on "Investment in Man."[27] And he contributed importantly to the development of the concept of "investment" and the methods of measurement not only by his own research, but by the research he encouraged. Gary Becker, in his volume, *Human Capital,* explored in greater depth than others the concepts of educational investment and the measurement of the rate of educational returns.[28] Becker, in a quantitative study restricted to white males, after personal taxes, shows a private rate of return from high school graduation rising from 16 percent in 1939 to 28 percent in 1958. Returns as measured are private rates of return and relate to earnings attributable to high school graduation, but do not take account of other future satisfactions. Others, including Mary Jean Bowman, W. Lee Hansen, Burton Weisbrod, and Jacob Mincer are among those whose research deepened the concept of human capital formation through education and returns from the investments made.

Education as an investment clearly has long-term consequences for the level and changes in economic growth. Major studies of education as a source of growth and the measurements of outcome in growth have been linked, however, to the analyses of the "residual" or unexplained growth in GNP—a growth not attributable to conventionally defined inputs. Edward F. Denison's important study of sources of growth quantified earnings differentials from years of schooling and the national income growth consequence of those added years of school. (Denison adjusts somewhat arbitrarily for "ability" to get at the pure effects of schooling.) Denison's findings for the period 1950-1962 are that education (again measured by earnings differences attributable to years of schooling but adjusted downward for ability-effects) explains about 15 percent of the total 3.36 percent per annum GNP growth rates.[29] Jorgenson and Griliches,[30] in a study of productivity change, specified labor quality inputs into a model of growth in value added.

In Griliches' study of manufacturing and determinants of state differences in value added in manufacturing using a labor quality variable, results showed education to have strong explanatory effects on value added. The longitudinal analysis of gross product from manufacturing found rates of growth in income 3.22 percentage points a year, with schooling per man accounting for .73 percentage points or 23 percent. Labor quality is defined essentially as educational inputs into the productive system. And in the use of education (years of schooling) as a proxy variable, new issues come to be raised concerning the way in which education impacts on growth or value added. (All these approaches assume that years of schooling are reflective of education as the investment, and yields are assumed to be earnings reflective of productivity and productivity, of skill acquired.)

Specification of measurements of investment outcomes and quantification of those outcomes in the past have assigned little income return in investment in education of mothers who do not enter the paid work force. The notion of investment in education for child motivation and learning generates still an additional postponed return. While explicit recognition of investment for parental involvement in the education of the child has received little attention aside from some work by Levin, Bowman, and this author, returns to the education of the woman who chooses to stay at home and raise her family are important for child learning and have a number of educational policy implications.

In summary, these several approaches involve primarily determination of earnings differentials attributable to years (or quality) of education. And they point to a factoring out of "native" ability (without due regard to the creation of ability by education). While essentially the measurements developed in the conceptual work that has been done are of the macro type that is not readily used in micro analysis requiring comparing of results from activity options for a school district or school, there are aspects of the measurements that are applicable to performance evaluation. Performance payments in an investment context would mean payments for graduating a young person from high school, or payments related to some yardstick of skill created or earnings differentials created through educational services.

Some Concluding Observations

The built-in incentive structure of performance contracting should help us gain much knowledge about the efficacy of contractual payments as an incentive. Essentially, we are learning whether performance contracting is beneficial or, rather, if it achieves what it is designed to achieve, and to what degree or in what measure it does work, and under what circumstances. Performance rests on the outcome sought. End results are the critical testing grounds.

What criteria are to be used in measuring success? The four A's—aptitude, achievement, attitude, and attribute—presented in this paper are indicative of the multidimensional products of concern in education. Most research in the past has centered on aptitudes and achievements. Standardization of tests, updating of their norms, and wider application to assure general usefulness continue to necessitate major additional efforts. The achievement target of insuring a year's progress for every year of school for every pupil is not possible of attainment. Some children cannot meet that target without an inordinate input of resources. Further, programmed instruction has made plain that norm-referenced tests are not a substitute for the specifics of reading or numbering achievement, for example, learning a defined number of words of defined characteristics and designation.

Much less developed are the measures of attributes and attitudes. Many different measurements have been formulated, and at least experimentally some have been tried on small population groups. National assessment has undertaken to include in its testing program attitudinal tests related to curriculum matter. But much additional research is needed. We can start to apply one or two known testing instruments on samples of national population or on a statewide basis and improve the measurements as experience is gathered. Or we can wait and opt for more research as a prior condition to application of concept and instrument. A range of questions on both direct effects and on feedback could with profit be the subject of research for purposes of fact gathering for educational programming. However, a beginning on application may well clarify the need for an acceleration of the research on outcomes.

Quality alone measured by the four A's is but one aspect among many in that complex product we call education.

Notes

1. Jesse Burkhead. *Input and Output in Large-City High Schools.* Syracuse, New York: Syracuse University Press, 1967.
2. James S. Coleman, *et al. Equality of Educational Opportu-*

nity. Washington, D.C.: U.S. Department of Health, Education, and Welfare, Office of Education (OE-38001), 1966.

3. Irene Athey and Duane O. Rubadeau. (eds.) *Educational Implications of Piaget's Theory.* Waltham, Massachusetts: Ginn and Company, 1970.

4. Jerome Bruner. (ed.) *Learning About Learning: A Conference Report.* Washington, D.C.: U.S. Department of Health, Education, and Welfare, Office of Education (OE-12019), 1966.

5. Joseph A. Kershaw. *Government Against Poverty.* Washington, D.C.: The Brookings Institution, 1970, p. 67.

6. Jerome S. Bruner. *The Process of Education.* New York: Vintage Books, 1960.

7. J. Floud. *Ability and Educational Opportunity.* Report of an OECD Conference organized in collaboration with the Swedish Ministry of Education. Kungalv, Sweden, June 1961.

8. Lawrence A. Cremin. *The Transformation of the Schools.* New York: Vintage Books, 1961.

9. Edward L. Thorndike. The Nature, Purposes, and General Methods of Measurements of Educational Products, in National Society for the Study of Education, *Seventeenth Yearbook.* Bloomington, 1918; Part II, p. 16.

10. Educational Policies Commission. *Education for All American Youth.* Washington, D.C.: 1944, p. 21.

11. Nolan C. Kearney. *Elementary School Objectives.* New York: Russell Sage Foundation, 1953, p. 166.

12. Quoted by Richard M. Jaegar in *A National Test Equating Study in Reading* (unpublished, undated).

13. Remarks by The Honorable E.L. Richardson before the National Education Association, Detroit, Michigan, June 29, 1971.

14. John P. Robinson and Phillip R. Shaver. *Measures of Social Psychological Attitudes* (Appendix B to *Measures of Political Attitudes*). Ann Arbor, Michigan: Survey Research Center,

Institute for Social Research, The University of Michigan, August 1969.

15. John P. Robinson, Jerrold G. Rusk, and Kendra B. Head. *Measures of Political Attitudes.* Ann Arbor, Michigan: Survey Research Center, Institute for Social Research, The University of Michigan, August 1968.

16. For example, see G. Lester Anderson. Recommendations of the Mid-Century Committee on Outcomes in Elementary Education—Their Implications for Research in Education Psychology. Paper presented at Symposium of the American Psychological Association, September 1952.

17. Quoted in R.B. Cattell and H.J. Butcher. *The Prediction of Achievement and Creativity.* Indianapolis: The Bobbs-Merrill Co., 1968.

18. R.B. Cattell and Herbert W. Eber. *Handbook for the Sixteen Personality Factor Questionnaire.* Champaign, Illinois: IPAT, 1968.

19. Goal Attainment Scaling Project, directed by Dr. Thomas Kiresuk, Chief Clinical Psychologist and Director of Program Evaluation, Hennepin County Health Center, Minneapolis, Minnesota; in progress.

20. William H. Angoff. (ed.) *The College Board Admissions Testing Program.* A Technical Report on Research and Development Activities Relating to the Scholastic Aptitude Test and Achievement Tests. New York: College Entrance Examination Board, 1971.

21. A. Gleason and E. Begle. Notes on Plenary Sessions: Mathematics: Discussion with A. Gleason and E. Begle—Second Generation Math Project, in Jerome Bruner: *Learning About Learning.* Washington, D.C.: U.S. Department of Health, Education, and Welfare, Office of Education, 1966, pp. 267-269.

22. Alice M. Rivlin. *Systematic Thinking for Social Action.* Washington, D.C.: The Brookings Institution, 1971.

23. Samuel Bowles. *Planning Education Systems for Economic Growth.* Cambridge: Harvard University Press, 1969.
24. Ivar Berg. *The Great Training Robbery.* New York: Praeger Publishers, 1970.
25. Mary Jean Bowman. Education and Economic Growth, in National Education Finance Project: *Economic Factors Affecting the Financing of Education.* Gainesville, Florida: The NEF Project, 1970, p. 110.
26. Kelvin Lancaster. In *American Economic Review: Papers and Proceedings,* May 1966.
27. T.W. Schultz. Reflections on Investment in Man. *Journal of Political Economy,* Vol. 2, part 2, Supplement, October 1962, pp. 1-8.
28. Gary S. Becker. *Human Capital.* New York: Columbia University Press, 1964.
29. Edward F. Denison. The Sources of Economic Growth in the United States. Supplementary Paper No. 13. New York: Committee for Economic Development, 1962. And also, *Why Growth Rates Differ.* Washington, D.C.: The Brookings Institution, 1967.
30. D.W. Jorgenson and Z. Griliches. The Explanation of Productivity Change. *Review of Economic Studies,* Autumn 1967, *34,* pp. 249-283.

The research on which this paper draws was carried out under contract to the Public Services Laboratory from the National Center for Educational Statistics (OEC-0-70-4454 [521]).

7.

Employment Relations Under Performance Contracting

MYRON LIEBERMAN

In a paper dealing with policy issues, it is often helpful if an author reveals his biases, however tentative they be. In this case, I do so gladly; my view is that objectivity consists not in concealing one's real preferences, but in articulating them fully, so that others are better able to evaluate their impact on the conduct of a study. With this in mind, let me state my initial biases relating to employment relations and performance contracting.

1. Performance contracting is a potentially significant innovation in education, with better long- than short-term prospects for bringing about basic reforms in education.

2. Collective bargaining and strong teacher organizations are desirable as a matter of public policy. The rationale for them is stronger in public education, and in public employment generally, than it is for collective bargaining and strong unions in the private sector. This rationale is essentially a conservative view, having little or nothing to do with the impact of collective bargaining upon the salaries or benefits of the employees concerned. In my view, arbitrary or discriminatory governmental action is an ever-present danger. Individual citizens or individual public employees are

Myron Lieberman is Director, Office of Program Development and Administration (Teacher Education), City University of New York.

119

typically ineffective in resisting such undesirable governmental action. Unless there exist strong organizations, relatively free from government control, and ready, willing, and able to require public officials to explain and defend their actions, there are unacceptable risks of inefficient, corrupt, and discriminatory government. Such organizations may on occasion prove to be a troublesome obstacle to desirable government action, but the advantages of having such organizations far outweigh the disadvantages.

3. In the long run, the extent to which performance contracting is used, and fulfills its potential, will depend upon the effectiveness of public management. The opposition to performance contracting by teacher organizations may be a decisive factor in its rejection by some districts; but over the long haul, the future of performance contracting is up to school management.

4. Employment relations is an extremely important dimension of performance contracting. In fact, this assumption was a decisive factor in my decision to investigate the topic.

My sympathetic view toward performance contracting has many roots. As a resident of New York City, I pay more in state and local taxes than I would anywhere else in the United States. When the city administration asserts, as mine has lately, that sanitation workers in the *private* sector are three times as efficient as those in the uniformed services, and that the city could save a great deal by contracting out garbage collection, my reaction was "Why not do it, instead of just talking about it?"

A few years ago, a close friend of mine accepted employment with one of the country's leading land developers. In discussing this firm, my friend was especially impressed by the effectiveness of the firm's procedures for deciding whether or not to contract out certain tasks, such as publications. Since then, I have been especially interested in school board policies on the subject. My impressionistic judgment is that very few school boards, if any, have thought about subcontracting systematically. Work such as running a cafeteria, busing students, or maintenance is sometimes contracted out, but system operations are not analyzed systematically for their contracting-out possibilities. Since policies which have not been analyzed critically often provide fertile ground for reform, I was—and still am—prepared to accept the possibility of dramatic improvements through some form of contracted instructional services.

Finally, and to remove any possible doubts on an attitudinal matter which often dominates current discussion of performance contracting, let me repeat a comment which I have repeatedly affirmed since it first appeared in print over ten years ago:

> In one sense, I place myself with the "critics" of public education. I am convinced that our schools are not as effective as they should be. I mean by this more than the simple idea that improvement is possible. Improvements are possible in every social institution—our courts, our legislatures, our hospitals, and so on. When I cast my lot with the "critics," I mean to say that the return on our educational investment is too low to be brushed aside by sincere but routine admissions that improvement is possible and desirable. I am asserting that the gap between the achievable and the actual results of public education should be a matter for deep national concern and that this concern must not abate until the gap has been drastically reduced.*

Procedural Problems

Like some performance contractors, it appears that my

---

*Myron Lieberman. *The Future of Public Education.* Chicago: The University of Chicago Press, 1960, p. 13.

performance was not equal to my intentions. This paper admittedly lacks the empirical base for an adequate assessment of employment relations under performance contracting. I have read performance contracts, position papers, and articles on the subject. I have talked to a variety of sources on a variety of issues relating to employment relations under performance contracting. Unfortunately, the task proved to be much more complex than was originally anticipated.

For example, in one district, a teacher organization representative presented me with documents and arguments to the following effect:

1. The superintendent wanted to participate in the OEO projects to enhance his image as an innovator, and thereby persuade a new board to retain him.

2. His successor, who was black, embraced the project as a source of patronage, loading the staff with unqualified persons.

3. The project was advocated publicly as a means of getting rid of, or overcoming, white teachers who didn't care about black students.

4. Teachers' representatives coming to a meeting to resolve the problems were met with pickets labeling the teacher representatives as racists.

Now, these and other allegations are serious matters. However, in order to assess them adequately, and to be fair to others involved, it would have been necessary to interview the district board and administrators, the project staff, the paraprofessionals employed, teachers in and out of the project, OEO personnel, and others in a position to contribute to an objective assessment. There were literally dozens of situations where such procedures would have been required to deal with the gut issues. Unfortunately, I was not able to utilize such procedures, much as I would have preferred, and as valuable as the study might be if conducted this way.

The difficulty of getting the facts was not confined to assessing conflicting accounts of empirical events. For what it may be worth, only a few school districts, contractors, and/or teacher organizations returned copies of the performance contracts. I recognize the time and effort which may be involved, especially since the parties undoubtedly received many such requests, but the impression left is hardly an attractive one. When school districts send fancy brochures extolling the virtues of a performance contract, but cannot seem to find copies of the contract itself, which is a public document, some skepticism is inevitable. This is especially true when the demand for copies should have been anticipated.

Another problem is that there is so much discussion of performance contracts in terms of assumptions or specific practices which are not inherently related to performance contracts. For instance, consider the following quotation from a position paper on performance contracts:

> One of the manifestations of the current call for accountability in the public schools is the concept of performance contracting. It is most simply defined as an educational experience in which a private corporation contracts for classroom instruction.*

This quotation confuses the concept of performance contracts with the concept of subcontracting, a very pervasive and unfortunate confusion in the literature and discussion of perform-

---

A Statement of Position and Suggested Guidelines on Performance Contracting adopted by the 1971 Spring Representative Assembly East Lansing, Michigan: Michigan Education Association, 1971, p. 1.

ance contracting. Some of the most perceptive and most adamant opponents of performance contracting per se explicitly stated that their opposition was not to subcontracting but to performance contracting.

Issues in Employment Relations
Under Performance Contracts

Let me now turn to some of the basic issues relating to employment relations under performance contracts, or as they might be affected by performance contracts. Some of these issues antedate performance contracting, but performance contracting has generated greater interest and greater pressure to clarify them.

Merit Pay

Merit pay is defined here as a procedure for compensation which distinguishes between two or more individuals doing the same kind of work on the basis of real or alleged differences in the quality or the output of the work performed. Salary differentials based upon different job descriptions, such as would be forthcoming under differentiated staffing, are not "merit pay" as just defined.

Teacher organizations have been opposed to merit pay for many decades. It is not surprising, therefore, that they opposed performance contracting on this basis. Nevertheless, logically and practically, the issue of merit pay for individual teachers or other employees under performance contracts is irrelevant to the concept of performance contracts. That is, performance contracts can be introduced in a meaningful way without merit pay. Of course, a district may wish to introduce performance contracts in a way which includes merit pay. Unfortunately, however, the evils or alleged evils of merit pay have already been tied to performance contracts per se in ways that could and should have been avoided.

In this connection, some of the supporters of performance contracts have been their own worst enemy, insofar as employment relations are concerned. Compensation for policemen, firemen, sanitation workers, and a host of other public employees (by far the majority) is not geared, collectively or individually, to results or to merit pay, as is envisaged by some kinds of performance contracts. Furthermore, it is fallacious to assume that most employees in private employment or the professions are paid this way. For example, the vast majority of employees in unions (about 20 million) are paid on the basis of services as rendered, not on the output or benefit of services as received.

The professions present a mixed picture. If your lawyer wins a case with a large award, he is apt to bill you on the basis of the benefits actually received by the client, i.e., services as received. If you lose, the lawyer doesn't; he bills you for his time, i.e., for his services as rendered. Similarly, a physician may charge a great deal for a little effort when he saves a life by fast action. By contrast, when the patient dies, the physician merely shifts his bill to a services as rendered basis.

In any case, it is inaccurate to assert that most people in our economy are paid according to results. Perhaps they should be. Be that as it may, I am already unequivocally on record to the effect that compensation in education can and should be related to productivity in a meaningful way. However, I question whether the way to do this is to give the impression that teachers are the major exception to the principle of basing compensation upon productivity, or that teachers constitute an exceptional pocket of resistance to the idea. Furthermore, there is a world of difference between gearing the compensation of a group of employees to the productivity of the group, and gearing the compensation of individual employees to individual measures of productivity. Some teacher opposition to performance contracting (how much is difficult to say) could (and in my judgment should) have been avoided by a clear-cut recognition of the distinction at the outset, coupled with an explicit avoidance of merit pay. Such avoidance need not have been permanent for those who regard merit pay as vitally important. As matters stand, however, there is nothing in the theory or practice of merit pay under performance contracting which differs significantly from approaches already rejected by teacher organizations, as by most organized employee groups.

The preceding comments should not be interpreted to mean that merit pay is a permanently hopeless proposition. I would like to suggest, however, that the basic problems of teacher compensation lie elsewhere, and that performance contracts, at least in their present form, are not likely to contribute much to the resolution of these problems. Let me elaborate on this point briefly.

A physician who does not keep abreast of developments in his field runs serious risks. For example, if a certain drug is found to have harmful effects in certain kinds of patients, and the fact is publicized in the medical literature, the physician may be guilty of negligence or malpractice for failure to act on the information. Similarly, lawyers and accountants are under constant pressure to keep abreast of developments in their fields. Even where malpractice is not an issue, the relationship between the professional's information and his appeal to clients is too obvious to be ignored.

In education, there is no such pressure on teachers to stay abreast of their field. The overwhelming majority of teachers are on a salary schedule and paid on the basis of years of education and experience. A teacher can continue to use outmoded methods for years without the slightest pressure from anyone. The problem is not that teachers don't care. It is that the compensation structure of education does not offer the rewards, and does not put much pressure, or pressure of any kind, on teachers to stay abreast of professional developments.

Changing this structure will be an enormously difficult and complex task, to say the least. Prima facie, it seems that the change would have to be preceded by a clear-cut demonstration of the superiority of teachers and of instructional systems which utilize what is known about the way to get the job done. Demonstrations which bog down in the finer points of measurement are not likely to provide the political base which is necessary for effective innovation.

None of the performance contracts known to me really address themselves to this structural problem. In fact, they may even exacerbate the problem in the long run. At best, successful contractors will turnkey in the optimum level of expertise at any given time. This is not to be denigrated, especially in a field where so many practitioners perform at a primitive level. The problem is that in the absence of a continuous relationship between the professional's information system and his compensation, what is turnkeyed is likely to prevail in the system for a long time to come. This is fine as long as new and better procedures are not developed. Suppose, however, that after all the travail in a particular district, there is improvement and something gets turnkeyed into the system. Suppose further that something even better comes down the pike the following year. Will the superintendent go to the board to request a *new* performance contract, contemplating a *new* turnkey operation? I doubt it very much.

Perhaps this is one of those problems, like how to spend a million, that we would like to have. Regardless, let me summarize by saying that it was unwise to inject the issue of merit pay into performance contracting. On the record to date, insofar as it is available to me, performance contracting has only kicked a sleeping dog, better left alone at this stage of development.

Differentiated Staffing

One of the basic weaknesses in the educational personnel structure is its lack of differentiation. Teachers differ by subject matter specialization; otherwise, there is relatively little differentiation by function (diagnostician, remediation, clinician, measurement, etc.). The teacher aide project at Bay City, Michigan in the 1950's was the forerunner of recent efforts to introduce some meaningful improvements in the educational personnel structure. "Team teaching" is a more recent effort characterized by considerable publicity and infinitesimal substance.

Performance contracts could move us much closer to developing a more productive personnel structure. However, if it is to avoid becoming another fiasco in the teacher aide and team teaching tradition, the use of paraprofessionals under performance contracts will have to follow a different path than the one taken to date. The different positions in the employment structure will have to be defined much more carefully, and related to training programs, educational facilities, and schedules in a rational way.

Thus far, no such development seems to be emerging from performance contracting. The projects under way present a mix of professional-paraprofessional relationships, but not one seems to be making it as a permanent feature of the educational personnel structure. At the same time, however, it is already apparent that any such development will present some extremely difficult problems of employment relationships. Let me list just a few of the basic questions which have already arisen and which would become matters of basic public and organizational policy if we develop a differentiated personnel structure.

- Should paraprofessionals have to be licensed?
- To what extent should paraprofessionals receive the same fringe benefits as teachers?

- Should paraprofessionals be in the same bargaining unit as teachers?
- Should paraprofessionals be represented by the same bargaining agent as teachers?
- Should organizational eligibility be the same for paraprofessionals and teachers?

The way in which such questions are resolved is of the utmost importance to education. Their importance is somewhat obscured where the contractor employs the paraprofessionals, but if a process is turnkeyed, the issues would emerge very quickly.

Significantly, the AFT and NEA are following different paths on this issue. The AFT is already making an intensive, and fairly successful, effort to organize paraprofessionals. Paradoxically, this approach was a consequence of the far-reaching confrontation between the UFT and certain black groups in New York's Ocean Hill-Brownsville in 1968-1969. On the other hand, the NEA has not made a firm decision at the national level to organize paraprofessionals; for a variety of reasons, there is more reluctance in NEA than in AFT to having the teacher organization organize paraprofessionals.

Consider some of the ramifications of this situation:

1. If paraprofessionals are not included in a bargaining unit, management is free to define the job and the terms and conditions of employment at management's discretion. If the paraprofessionals are in a bargaining unit, management has to bargain over terms and conditions of employment for paraprofessionals.

2. If paraprofessionals are in the same bargaining unit as teachers, what will be the implications and ramifications for membership in teacher organizations, for the racial composition and policies of the teacher organizations, and for the objectives of the combined organization at the bargaining table?

If the reader is interested in some of the dimensions of these problems, consider the following facts: In 1961, the UFT, in New York City had about 2,500 members. In 1971, it was the largest union local of *any kind* in the United States; I have been told that the UFT is the largest union local of any kind in the *world,* and this may well be the case. It is already larger than many international unions affiliated with the AFL-CIO, and it is probably going to get much larger in the near future.

For the most part, paraprofessionals employed by contractors have not posed serious problems for the bargaining agents. Some contractors have made a point of paying teachers and paraprofessionals the same as called for by the regular district contract. The point is, however, that the scope of unbridled managerial discretion relating to paraprofessionals is rapidly shrinking. Furthermore, we can expect the costs for paraprofessionals to rise in the near future, since their organizations will be under strong pressure from several sources to achieve dramatic gains for them.

The Profit Motive
Leaders of teacher organizations typically get and keep their positions chiefly because of their ability to achieve material benefits for their constituents—or to persuade them that this is happening, whether it is or not. We need not worry about the charges by such leaders that wanting to make money is an illegitimate motive to be in the education business. It may be a mistaken one, but it is no more inappropriate for a large corporation to enter the education market for profit, than for a person to decide to become a teacher—or teacher organization leader—for this reason. In short, criticism of performance contracts because the contractors want to make profits is irrelevant.

In this connection, a study of Peace Corps members has some

relevance. The study showed that members of the Peace Corps who joined because they saw something in it for themselves, as well as for humanity, typically served more effectively than those who joined solely for altruistic reasons. This makes sense and perhaps would not justify notice, except in education, where there is so much overemphasis on motives for becoming a teacher and so little attention to the factors that actually shape behavior on the job.

Of course, wanting to make money can lead to undesirable behavior. A restaurant owner may serve stale food. An automobile mechanic may get you to buy new parts that are not really needed. Lawyers may urge you to sue when you should settle, or vice versa. In all these and other situations, the sensible course is not to deny the dangers but to take the practical actions required to minimize them. Of course, the cost of protection against the dangers is a legitimate consideration in assessing a system of control, but I see no reason to regard the problem in performance contracting as too difficult or too costly to solve.

Of course, a common argument is that the profit motive leads contractors to make all sorts of promises that cannot be fulfilled. They raise false hopes and then resort to shady tactics or downright dishonesty (e.g., teaching to the test) to cash in on their promises.

Careless use of the term "guarantee" illustrates the way in which supporters of performance contracts have strengthened the credibility of their opponents. If there is a "guarantee," it is not that students will learn but that the contractor will not be paid if the students do not learn. One can argue that the typical "money back guarantee" in the commercial world means only no payment if there is no performance, but this is ingenuous, to say the least. Surely, it is if we are talking about an experiment instead of a tested product. The semantics may have been effective in generating school board support, but they certainly have had a negative effect upon teachers.

Unfortunately, the invalid criticisms of performance contracting because it is based upon the profit motive have obscured some of the basic dynamics of the process. We, or at least I, do not know enough about how the contractors hope to profit from performance contracts as a long-range enterprise. Some contractors appear to regard performance contracts as a means of selling instructional materials in which they have a proprietary interest. Such a view might induce firms to assume larger risks than if each performance contract had to show a profit in its own right. From the standpoint of employment relations, these alternatives might affect the salaries or incentive payments to school district employees. In any case, we need to know a great deal more about the total economics of the situation (as distinct from the project account per se) from the contractors' point of view. Otherwise, we are not likely to achieve a realistic understanding of employment dynamics under performance contracting.

A related issue is what happens to the rates if contractors or individual employees make large profits or incentive payments. Such an outcome would undoubtedly create pressures to raise the required performance levels, both at the contractor and the individual employee level. Understandably, the setting of rates for bonus or incentive or even regular pay is a sensitive issue in employment relations; the parties are continuously striving to have them adjusted or readjusted to advance their interests. In education, little attention has been paid to this issue, perhaps because of the turnkey assumption. If school districts are going to incorporate the practices demonstrated by the performance contracts, and do so with their own employees, there is no need to be concerned about the size of the incentive payments. Furthermore, many districts are participating only because their own money is not involved. Under such circumstances, the amount of profits is a state or an OEO, not a local, concern.

The individual incentive payments present some different problems, but I encountered a surprising lack of concern about the rates involved. I attribute this not so much to the turnkey aspect as to the fact that performance contracts involve funds which the districts would otherwise not have.

Regardless of the success of current projects, measured in terms of pupil gains, there are difficult questions concerning *what* is to be turnkeyed. Perhaps this is simply a deficiency in my understanding or my research, but it is not at all clear to me *what* would be turnkeyed, assuming that districts wished to incorporate whatever led to "success" in the projects. It would be helpful if this were clarified in some way that went beyond vague generalities. As it is, the observation that it is not "the" system but the fact that the contractors have "a" system may have considerable validity.

Legislative Reform

It is already apparent that the laws requiring the presence of certified teachers have been an obstacle in some performance contracts. In my judgment, it is desirable that we revise the state laws requiring that certified teachers supervise students for the school day—or alternatively, enable persons certified at much lower educational levels to supervise children. Where the laws cannot be repealed, they should at least be amended to provide long range experimental situations involving noncertified personnel.

Teacher organizations will undoubtedly oppose such changes. For example, the policy statement of the Michigan Education Association on performance contracting states that:

Teachers, along with all other instructional personnel, must be appropriately certified in accordance with Michigan law . . . Students participating in any performance contracting project must be subject to all laws, rules, and regulations which pertain to attendance and pupil management in the state of Michigan.*

Nevertheless, teacher opposition to laws requiring that pupils be under the control of certified personnel during the entire school day is on weak theoretical as well as practical grounds. According to the conventional wisdom in these matters, the "professional" part of the teacher's task is "instruction." This view is usually accompanied by a very elastic and broad definition of "instruction," such as in the following statement by the AFT's Director of Research:

I would maintain that those tasks which relate to or involve learners in any way are, in essence, instructional. If a person performs such tasks as grading multiple-choice or true/false tests, maintaining order, and supervising children, he is performing instructional tasks, and, in effect, is a teacher of children . . . In defining and, hopefully, stabilizing the concept of a teacher, I would submit that a person involved with children to the extent that he has the opportunity to influence behavior operates, in essence, as a teacher.**

*A Statement of Position and Suggested Guidelines on Performance Contracting adopted by the 1971 Spring Representative Assembly, East Lansing, Michigan: Michigan Education Association, 1971, p. 3.

**Robert D. Bhaerman. Education's New Dualisms. Washington: American Federation of Teachers, n.d., p. 3.

The preceding quotation illustrates a point of view which should be corrected promptly. To see why, ask yourself what is the "professional" work of a physician. Sometimes it is diagnosis. That is, it may require the utmost skill and knowledge to diagnose an ailment. Once diagnosed, however, it may be that a nurse or even a secretary or the patient himself can carry out the appropriate prescription, e.g., taking one tablet every four hours.

In other situations, diagnosis is obvious, even to the layman. The patient's arm is broken, or his skin is burned. In such cases, the "professional" role, i.e., the one requiring expert skill and judgment, is not diagnosis, which may be obvious to everyone, but prescription or implementation of prescription. A technician is often able to test for cancer, but a physician is required if an operation is required.

It would be folly to decide *a priori* and apart from the realities of certain tasks what requires a trained physician and what can be done by nurse's aides, or by other paraprofessionals. Clearly, it would be foolish to decide that diagnosis must always be conducted by, or in the presence of, a physician. Similarly, it would be unwise to say that prescription must be conducted in such presence. Yet this is what we have done in education, with far less justification than our much looser controls over medical activities. Thus, there are situations wherein expertise is required to diagnose an educational deficiency; once diagnosed, however, a paraprofessional or any intelligent lay person can sometimes provide the remedy, e.g., simple drill on a particular skill. There are other situations in which the educational diagnosis may be obvious, but the remedy requires a very high degree of expertise. For this reason, we should avoid legal definitions of "teacher" which assume that their expertise necessarily falls in the area of instruction. By the same token, we ought also to drop these all-embracing definitions of "instruction," which seem more designed to protect teacher employment than to do anything else.

Even if the case for performance contracts is weak or nonexistent, a strong case remains for modifying the legislation requiring that teachers supervise students at all times. I believe, however, that such changes could be advocated in a way that would generate the support of teachers and teacher organizations (or at least neutralize their opposition), despite the maladroit way the issue has been publicized thus far.

In this connection, a more realistic attitude toward the custodial functions of schools may be in order. No one prefers schools to be merely custodial institutions, even for a limited part of the school day. Nevertheless, we may do better educationally by accepting some custodial functions for what they are than by continuing to insist that every second of every school day will be an enriching educational experience if only under the guidance of a certified teacher. It is conceivable that children would be better off educationally at age 6 if ages 3 to 5 had been spent in a center which was less than an elementary school but more than a babysitting operation. Nevertheless, we cannot just superimpose such centers upon the existing structure. Conceivably, we might finance such centers, at least in part, out of savings made possible by reducing the amount of unnecessary time elementary pupils are under the supervision of certified teachers. Experience in Canada and some other countries, with educational and literacy standards equal or superior to our own, but with significantly lower certification requirements, especially at the elementary levels, provides additional support for this argument. And to avoid an error which is frequently attributed to others in this paper, I hasten to add that excessive credential or licensing requirements characterize a wide range of occupations and are a pervasive phenomena in our society. Licensing requirements generally are coming under widespread legal attack for their discriminatory effects; in fact, OEO ought to explore this matter vigorously as a part of its ongoing mission.

Collective Bargaining and the
Contracting Out of Work

At the present time, a majority of the nation's teachers work pursuant to a collective bargaining agreement. Nevertheless, very few of these agreements specifically refer to performance contracting or the contracting out of work. If experience in the private sector is any guide, this is likely to change. References to contracting out are very common in collective bargaining agreements in the private sector. In addition, there is a wealth of literature on the subject; a recent bibliography on it runs to 58 pages.*

The few agreements in public education which do refer to the contracting out of work *support* rather than restrict management's rights to contract out. The following clause is illustrative:

> The Board's right to operate and manage the school system is recognized, including the determination and direction of the teaching force, the right to plan, direct, and control, initiate or discontinue school activities; to schedule classes and assign workloads; to determine teaching methods and subjects to be taught; to maintain the effectiveness of the school system; to determine teacher complement; to create, revise, and eliminate positions; to establish and require observance of reasonable rules and regulations; to select and terminate

*David M. Farrell. *The Contracting Out of Work: An Annotated Bibliography.* Kingston, Ontario: Industrial Relations Centre, Queen's University, 1965.

teachers; to discipline and discharge teachers for cause
and to contract or subcontract any of its work.*

Such clauses did not emerge from negotiations over contracting out. Rather they were simply copied from existing contracts
with a strong management rights clause. And, in general, although
teacher organizations will be submitting more proposals on
performance contracting, especially if and when performance
contracting increases, there is a surprising lack of activity relating
to contracting out at the bargaining table.

There are at least two reasons for the inactivity. One is that
relatively few teacher organizations with bargaining rights are
currently affected directly by performance contracts. It would
have been useful to interview organization leaders in each district
where both collective bargaining and performance contracting are
realities, to see what stance the organizations plan to take on the
subject at future bargaining sessions.

Another reason calls for some comment. In Michigan, where
teacher collective bargaining is more advanced than in any other
state, the Michigan Education Association and its affiliates appear
to be taking a moderate, albeit confused, position on performance
contracting. One reason is a recent decision of the Michigan
Employment Relations Commission in a case involving highway
employees. In effect, the commission ruled that it was an unfair
labor practice for a county highway commission to contract out
work which could be done by members of the bargaining unit,
without first bargaining on the subject. Teacher organization
leaders in Michigan apparently believe that there is no need at this
time for contractual protections relating to performance contracts.
In their view, school boards are legally precluded from contracting

*Article IIIA, *1970-1971 Agreement*, Campbellsport, Wisconsin, p. 2.

out the normal work of teachers until the boards have bargained over such action. Such bargaining is expected to provide the organizations with adequate opportunity to take protective measures. Regardless of whether this interpretation is sound, it will obviously be easier to introduce performance contracts where teachers do not have the protection of legislation according teachers bargaining rights. Hopefully, performance contracts will not be funded on this basis, tempting as it may be to do so in the short run.

Teacher Opposition Reconsidered

Teacher organization leaders have been strongly criticized for their opposition to the OEO projects in performance contracting. Such opposition allegedly reflects a narrow interest on their part in protecting the interests of their constituents, not an unselfish interest in improving education.

There is clearly some fear on the part of some teachers that performance contracting would lead to a loss of teacher jobs. This fear is more of a reaction to performance contracting propaganda than to the realities of its performance. Where are teachers—one teacher even—displaced because of the greater productivity or accountability demonstrated by performance contracting? The apparent inability of the districts to utilize performance contracting to point to one such case should be of much greater concern than teacher organizations overreacting to the non-disappearance of teaching jobs. After the millions spent on performance contracting to improve the efficiency of an enterprise with over two million employees, it is unnerving to discover that not a single teacher job has been eliminated as a result. Granted, there are other ways of increasing productivity, but the absence of any increased productivity this way must be regarded as a discouraging indication of the success of the program.

In some respects, it may be just as well. For the sake of discussion, assume that performance contracting had demonstrated ways for districts to achieve the same output with far fewer teachers. The question would immediately arise as to whose responsibility it would be to absorb the loss. The individual teachers? Should school districts pay severance pay or retraining allowances as an overhead cost of running a school system? Should the states and/or the federal government absorb the costs in some way as a matter of public policy? Or should there be some mix of these possibilities, or others not mentioned?

I am not sure what the right answer is, or even whether there is one, but surely the worst answer would be to have the excess teachers absorb the entire cost of their unemployment in whatever ways they can. Such a policy elsewhere virtually guarantees employee opposition to changes which could lead to greater productivity, and perhaps also to their displacement. In the long run, policies which emphasize the need to introduce efficiencies while assisting displaced individuals to meet the major burdens of displacement are likely to prove the most effective in facilitating greater productivity throughout our economy.

As asserted previously, performance contracting was unwisely advocated in some districts as a job-saving technique, thereby frightening teachers into premature and wholly unnecessary opposition to it. The fact is that we have some very recent and very relevant experience on how school districts handle opportunities to increase their productivity by releasing excess teachers; to put it mildly, the results do not inspire confidence in the ability of school management to deal with the problem.

My reference here is to the situation resulting from the constitutional decisions prohibiting racial segregation in public education. These decisions made it possible for school districts to save hundreds of millions of dollars by eliminating segregated facilities and segregated personnel. In fact, a very large number did not. In many cases, districts were virtually forced by the courts to adopt obvious economies. The most crucial point for present purposes is what happened in the area of employment relations. Thousands of districts implemented the reductions in staff with such blatant discrimination that even conservative Southern judges were constrained to call a halt, or a slowing down, in some cases. Under these circumstances, it is quite understandable why many teachers, white and black, react sensitively to suggestions that staff may be reduced. I do not assert that the opposition of teacher organizations to performance contracts is based upon their fear of discriminatory treatment in staff reductions. My point is that if and when performance contracting does point the way to genuine increases in productivity, if it ever does, there will still be some basic issues relating to implementation that cannot be dismissed as the self-serving opposition of a vested interest.

Perhaps one additional observation may be in order. In education, the first casualties of performance contracting are not likely to be teachers. They are much more likely to be those professors of education responsible for teaching the methods and materials courses. At least, that is the view of the Chairman of OE's National Committee on Program Priorities in Teacher Education (Dean Benjamin Rosner of the City University of New York), one of our most astute students of teacher education. I am inclined to agree with Rosner's analysis, disconcerting as it is to the established order.

Bear in mind that much of performance contracting is really intensive in-service teacher education. If private companies can contract with school districts and make a visible improvement in teacher performance within a relatively short period of time, our methods and materials experts are going to be confronted by some hard questions, e.g., what do we need you for when private enterprise can achieve demonstrable improvements which you have been unable to produce? It hasn't come to this yet, but it might.

Some Suggestions

One suggestion is that a number of school districts conduct an across-the-board analysis of their programs to ascertain which elements could be contracted out. For example, it seems impractical to me to train automotive mechanics in schools, since school facilities and personnel cannot keep pace with the changes in the automotive industry. Why not pay industry to provide the training, since it has by far the better personnel and facilities to do this particular job? Furthermore, not only would it be less expensive to use facilities which are already in place and used extensively, but the firms providing the training could introduce students to the world of work in a more direct and meaningful way.

Of course, this is not a new idea; in fact, it is already being implemented in some districts. However, unlike the OEO approach to date, I see no particular reason to emphasize reading and mathematics, or disadvantaged pupils in contracting out instructional tasks. My thought is to provide the local museums, dramatics clubs, symphony orchestras, dance societies, and other cultural and recreational agencies with an educational budget, so that they could carry on instructional programs currently regarded as school functions.

As a long-time tennis player, I have long been concerned about the small number of black children who get opportunities to play and become proficient in this sport. There are hundreds of Arthur Ashe's out there, if we could only provide the opportunities. Why not give children an option, whereby they can take tennis or golf lessons from private instructors at public expense, instead of attending regular gym or physical education classes? Such an approach might not result in "performance contracts" but in contracts for services rendered. Regardless, I think the average tennis professional is better able to teach tennis than the average physical education teacher, who is seldom a specialist in this particular sport.

In any case, I would like to emphasize two aspects of the suggestion. One is that controversies over performance contracts have tended to obscure the possibilities of less complicated contracts for instructional services. It is premature to say that performance contracts cannot be drawn up for instruction in music, art, dance, tennis, golf, or what have you. My guess is that they can be. However, they are very unlikely to be drawn up properly in individual districts, especially smaller ones, since the R & D expense in drawing up the contracts would be prohibitive. We need model performance contracts that can be used, with perhaps some modifications, by many districts. It should be emphasized, however, that the contracting out of some services should not be dependent upon the possibility of a performance contract per se. Performance contracts may eventually develop out of contracts for services, especially if there is dissatisfaction with the services rendered. At the same time, we should continue to explore the possibilities of contracted services that are short of performance contracts.

My second point may be crucial to the future of performance contracting. In the long run, some forms of performance contracts are bound to generate opposition from teacher organizations. If a contractor can instruct as effectively using technology or paraprofessionals instead of teachers, it is unrealistic to expect the teachers concerned to applaud the fact, however beneficial outsiders may think it is.

The problem here is that performance contracting propaganda has frightened teachers when it was completely unnecessary and counterproductive to do so, even assuming for the sake of argument that performance contracts will quickly demonstrate that we can do the job as well or better with fewer teachers. As argued elsewhere in this paper, education is inefficient, and shows little increase in productivity, partly because teachers have no direct stake in greater productivity. Clearly, one of the basic policy issues to be resolved is whether we are going to give teachers a direct stake in greater productivity, or whether we are going to discuss alleged or real gains in terms of getting rid of teachers or other terms which generate opposition instead of support. The principle should be that management can introduce efficiencies, but that excess employees shall have employment security, perhaps in new capacities or after some sort of training. A fundamental issue here is who should pay for such employment security—the local district, the state, or the federal government. As we move toward greater state and federal funding, perhaps these agencies will support a larger share of these costs.

The crucial point, however, is the strategy of community involvement in the contracts. At present, when performance contracting is introduced, it often encounters teacher opposition but generates no interest group support in the community. This is especially true where the contractor is an outside firm. The case would be much different if contracting were implemented along the lines suggested above. An imposing number of local organizations would have a direct and immediate stake in a contract for educational services. This may create some new problems while solving the one under discussion, but the options ought to be clear. At least, the suggested approach may be as viable in some districts as those currently supported. Certainly, there are enough districts with competent leadership ready, willing, and able to try it out.

Let me now suggest another contracting possibility with basic implications for employment relations. I tend to agree with the view that secondary schools are playing custodial roles more than they should. Some of our New York City schools do not even play a custodial role very well; in some schools, only 25 to 50 percent out of the register attend on any given day, and it is a different group from day to day. Unfortunately, our diagnosis, and hence our prescription, for this state of affairs is faulty. We do not adequately relate the diagnosis to the facilities or to the location of schools; hence we are not realistic about the measures needed to solve the problem.

In May, a high school senior is likely to be in class from 8:30 to 3:00, five days a week. In September as a college freshman, he is likely to be in class about 15 hours a week. The college schedule permits a student to go to the library, work, get something to eat, watch TV, and so on, without direct supervision. Because students are in class much less, it is easier to avoid custodial functions while they are in class.

To illustrate the high school problem, suppose a student wants to take a private music lesson or see a doctor during his study period. Ordinarily, this cannot be done, because the student would lose too much time traveling between classes. Suppose, however, that when we built new schools, we also constructed commercial facilities across the street. These commercial facilities could be rented to a wide assortment of specialists—educational, medical, and otherwise. Private teachers of music, dance, and art would be located in the complex. Pediatricians and dentists specializing in children's problems could also be there. That is, such personnel would be there if there was such a facility and if it was known that pupils could leave school for private lessons or services during the day. The pupil who can't get specialized instruction because he doesn't want to miss school or be absent from work, or because he lacks convenient transportation would no longer lose these opportunities. Similarly, many other students would benefit from the opportunities which could be provided this way.

These suggestions raise a question concerning the OEO projects. Should they be viewed as experiments in educating the disadvantaged, or as educational experiments with promise for any level or subject matter? As a matter of logic, the experiments can be viewed as either or both. Strategically, however, the emphasis is crucial. In view of OEO's mission, it was inevitable that its projects were motivated by a sincere desire to educate the disadvantaged effectively. The approach made good sense from some other standpoints as well; but, in retrospect, it may have been a mistake. For one thing, it tends to tie performance contracting to the disadvantaged and to lend credence to the charges that performance contracts per se are a copout on the part of public officials with responsibility for educating the disadvantaged. More importantly, it has tended to limit an idea with extremely broad ramifications. Consider the following language from a bill intended to authorize performance contracting in the state of New York:

> 36. In its discretion, during each of the school years 1971-1972, 1972-1973, 1973-1974, to enter into performance guarantee contracts with private contractors for the purpose of experimentation to increase the achievement level of students in grades kindergarten through twelve who have not achieved predetermined goals in reading and mathematics under existing methods presently employed by public schools.*

*Proposed Senate Bill 573-B, Cal. No. 419, prefiled January 6, 1971, introduced by Senator Thomas Laverne, Chairman, Standing Committee on Education, Senate of the State of New York.

New York education law has been interpreted to restrict performance contracting to certain situations specified by law. It may be that Senator Laverne, who is an astute politician as well as a dedicated legislator, felt that it was necessary to limit performance contracting if there was to be any chance of expanding its eventual use in the state. Even in such a case, however, it was probably a tactical mistake to start with such a limited approach.

Concluding Remarks

My own view is that the greatest benefit of performance contracting is its thrust toward the formulation of educational objectives and their analysis in terms of costs in a practical way. The following quotation seems as appropriate today as when I first wrote it in 1959:

> The problem . . . is that the teachers have failed to establish sets of intermediate objectives which would clarify how they propose to fulfill the general objectives of education. The discussion of objectives is usually concerned with the general ones, but this is not where the problem lies. It lies in establishing consistent, defensible, and attainable intermediate objectives which can serve as the basis for evaluating the progress made by the profession.*

Let me conclude, however, by emphasizing two points concerning objectives. The first is that they are primarily a management responsibility. School management, not teacher organizations, bears the primary responsibility for the absence of

*Myron Lieberman. *The Future of Public Education.* Chicago: University of Chicago Press, 1960, p. 21.

practical objectives in education.

Secondly, it should be stressed that the problem of setting and adjusting defensible objectives is not peculiar to education. It is, in fact, a pervasive problem of government at all levels. As one of the country's most brilliant urbanologists asserted recently:

> I know of at least a hundred cities that have had studies made of trends in their local economy and other basic life-support systems. Perhaps another hundred cities can be found that have attempted to establish goals. But I have yet to find a city that tries to spell out in clear, operational terms just what life could be like if the city could achieve its objectives and reverse undesirable trends or reinforce desirable ones. We expend our energies on diagnosis and prescription and never get around to describing how the results would look, feel, and act. In short, we have no clear *vision* of the good life to which people can relate effort, sacrifice, costs, and benefits.*

My hope is that performance contracting will constitute a major step toward solving the problem delineated by Molinaro. If our educational efforts are successful, what will pupils know, and what will they be able to do? If performance contracting can move us toward raising and answering these questions in a practical way, it will be a constructive development, regardless of its shortcomings on other grounds.

---

*Leo A. Molinaro. Truths and Consequences for Older Cities. *Saturday Review*, May 15, 1971, p. 30.

8.

Conclusions

I

Four major conclusions seem to have emerged from the preceding papers and from discussions of the papers at the Conference:

1. At this time, the precise impact of performance contracting on student achievement is unclear, and it may remain so for a period of years, or at least until the major technical and operational problems of student performance measurement are resolved. Yet the performance contracting approach seems to have exciting potential for school system innovation, more rational educational management and resource allocation, clearer and more persistent setting of objectives, and the development of more useful performance measures. Performance contracting ultimately may prove important for strictly non-pedagogical reasons.

2. Any comprehensive or summary evaluations of performance contracting at this time and in the future must recognize its diverse applications and benefits by employing a range of measures in addition to those related directly to the objectives of student achievement. Such evaluation must consider not only classroom effectiveness, but also a broad range of effects. In addition, it will be useful to consider the impact of performance contracting on the rate, content, and effects of school system change and to evaluate the ability of performance contracting to expand the

number of tools and agents that public schools can use to achieve their objectives.

3. The private sector probably does have much to contribute to public education, especially in training programs. Yet it is not certain that performance contracting is the best way to elicit and implement this contribution.

4. Regardless of the fate of the performance contracting movement, we must not lose sight of the larger issue of contracting itself. There seems to be much potential in some form of contracting for certain public education functions, whether or not the contract in question includes very tight performance specifications and a variable payment schedule.

Donald M. Levine
Conference Chairman

II

Performance contracting and turnkey operations were originally designed to be a catalyst for school system renewal. The criteria for assessing their success must include the following: a means by which to introduce cost-effectiveness programs in areas such as math and reading; a low-risk, low-cost vehicle for experimentation; an opportunity to increase community involvement in both planning and operations; an opportunity to rationalize the collective bargaining processes; a politically acceptable and educationally effective means to ensure school system integration *or* to provide "equity of education results" in those situations where neighborhood school feelings are strong; and a means for humanizing the classroom for both teacher and learner.

As a low-risk, low-cost vehicle for experimentation and catalyst for change, performance contracting combined with effective turnkey applications has been judged to be successful. Whether or not it provides more cost-effective instruction is less clear. Recent analyses of achievement data in the Virginia project indicate that it was much more cost-effective than originally thought; "homegrown projects" such as those in Grand Rapids have been very successful. On the other hand, projects implemented with a short lead time constrained by evaluation design criteria have posed operational problems indicating only scattered success.

Because of school-firm interface problems, many of the OEO projects had very little chance of success after the first month or so of operations when these problems arose.

Regarding the other criteria for judging performance contracting, it is just too early to tell. There exists a definite need for new evaluation designs and testing instruments to be developed and implemented in long-range projects such as that in Gary, Indiana.

Performance contracting in its "first generation" form should put itself out of business because of its success, spinning off hybrid versions—in Dade County, where individual teachers have entered into contracts with the school board with the possibility of earning a $5,000 bonus; or the Accountability Model in Michigan where school districts could receive $200 for every child who achieves specified levels while providing the district the flexibility to spend the money any way desired and yet encouraging them to search the market place for the most cost-effective systems.

Much of the data presently available for analysis has been contaminated by the controversial nature of performance con-

tracting, which may be an implicit compliment alone. Never in the
history of public education have so *few* groups with so *little*
resources done so *much* to frighten—unjustifiably, I feel—so *many*
educators.

Charles L. Blaschke
President
Education Turnkey Systems, Inc.

III

Impassioned controversy has marked the blazing half-life of
performance contracting. Educators at all levels have been quick
to throw stones or raise banners. But there is little doubt that
knowledge and education for the moment are at discount in the
United States. This is the result of the unforeseen consequence of
the use of knowledge, and not less frequently, of the presumption
of knowledge where perhaps none existed previously. It becomes
difficult to admit to ignorance and easy to assume the reliability
of information that is anything but reliable. An old saying held
that "it is not ignorance that hurt so much as knowing all those
things that ain't so." The schools have been more than a little hurt
of late by that phenomenon, and this, too, has deepened the sense
of under-achievement or even of failure of the schools to serve
their purpose in our time.

But it is true that certain costly school programs introduced
with great expectations a few years ago are not yielding the
promised or expected results. In fact the entire concept of a
clear-cut positive cost-quality relationship in education has been

called into question by recent reports. Increasingly educators are hearing that there first must be hard evidence that a proposed program offers the most effective solution available and a tangible return to the taxpayers before more funds will be put into it. Citizens are saying that the nation is not getting as much out of its investment in public education as it should for the dollars expended. Increasingly we hear the charge that the gap between educational promise and performance is a function of the outpourings of propaganda by the professional education community, and the persistent failure of educational leaders to produce implicitly promised results.

Performance contracting is not new in education. Deleterious effects of such contracts are described in the *Canadian Educational Monthly* of 1881. Its current popularity in the United States is responsive to a demand for greater accountability. The present performance contracting programs represent only a fraction of the variety possible. This potential for almost infinite variation is the real strength of "performance contracting," and the improvement of the educational system demands that its potential be fully explored. This suggests that all performance contracting must be evaluated from a broad perspective. Faults will be discovered in any program, but the attempt must be made to determine whether the faults are the result of that program, that contract and that contractor, or whether, on the other hand, the faults stem from basic defects in the performance contracting concepts. If the evaluative effort focuses merely on the amount of the achievement gained and the payment the contractor earns, much of the information obtainable from the experience will be lost.

Like any change in the style and substance of operation, this most recent venture into performance contracting involves problems for education. Tracing the complex and involved interconnections by which "inputs" produce "outputs" in an endeavor as large as public education is not the work of amateurs. It is not yet being done successfully in any other area of our national life, save in economics, and there most economists would insist that it is being done imperfectly. It is not being done elsewhere because no one really knows how to do it. It is just that most persons who have considered the matter feel it has to be done and accordingly someone will have to learn how to do it. Perhaps many someones. That, in short, is what this conference on performance contracting was all about.

George B. Brain
Dean, College of Education
Washington State University

IV

While I understand the conditions which gave rise to the experiment, I question the propriety of school systems contracting with private firms to perform the basic function for which schools have been organized and supported. Even so, I sense the desperation in some quarters which led to such a practice. I have reservations about the narrowness of contract objectives but I also have concerns about school administrators and teachers who seem incapable of specifying what they are about. I think measurement problems are being ignored and that they must be dealt with or payment by results becomes a hoax.

Much of this seems negative, but I am not completely negative. When I visited the contract sites, I found many of the teachers and paraprofessionals interested and apparently effective. I also found that pupils who were in contract programs could be rather explicit about what they were doing, how they were achieving, and, for the most part, they seemed interested in the program activities. Some of this interest might be ascribed to the novelty of the program or to the mechanical devices used. Perhaps even more important was the attention now centered on the pupils, possibly for the first time in their school careers.

Despite the limitations of the experiment, we can learn a great deal from it. It seems clear that the achievement of youngsters in reading and other basic skills is a concern at all levels of our society. Moreover, if that concern appears to be inadequately dealt with at local and state levels, it will get attention at the national level. Again, in the contracting experience the insistence of the larger society on an accounting by one of its social institutions, the schools, is exemplified. The focus of contracts on ends reminds us that we are concerned about means as well as ends, that both process and outcome are of vital importance to the educational enterprise.

Roald F. Campbell
Fawcett Professor of
Educational Administration
Ohio State University

V

The survival and, in most cases, the expansion in 1971-1972 of programs derived from the performance contracting efforts of the previous year support my belief that performance contracting has facilitated the introduction of needed changes in the instructional process. Specifically, classroom atmospheres are more salutary and instruction is more appropriate to students' needs and interests. The emphasis of performance contracting on student learning was also highly desirable and has helped focus attention where it belongs.

An apparent disadvantage of performance contracting, its dependence on norm-referenced tests for measuring program effectiveness, is also having beneficial effects. The inadequacy of such tests for the task was so strongly highlighted by the programs of 1970-1971 that valuable new efforts to construct more suitable instruments have been stimulated.

Unfortunately, the future of performance contracting is not promising. Its failure may derive from two misconceptions on the part of both contractors and school personnel. First, there was an expectation that there are quick solutions to the long-standing problems of the educationally disadvantaged. Second, despite their innovative thrusts, the performance contracting programs may still have been too much in the institutional mold, especially in the way they used people and time. Much more radical changes may well be needed to make education of the disadvantaged effective.

Polly Carpenter
Senior Staff Member
The Rand Corporation

VI

If the difficulties encountered by some pupils in learning were due mainly to incompetence or poor motivation of their teachers, and if the achievements desired of them could be defined clearly and completely, and assessed categorically as attained or not attained, then performance contracting would offer a promising alternative to conventional schooling. But the educational situations in which these conditions prevail are not frequently encountered. Hence it is unreasonable to expect performance contracting to yield substantial educational benefits.

The difficulties of validly assessing the effectiveness of performance contracting in practical school situations are formidable. Some reports may overstate, some may understate its actual effectiveness. Experience over several years is likely to provide better evidence than a one-shot evaluation of the initial trial.

I do not expect to find in 1975 that more than a very small proportion (1 or 2 percent) of the instruction in public schools is being offered under performance contract.

Robert L. Ebel
Professor of Education
and Psychology
Michigan State University

VII

Experience with performance contracting during 1970-1971 indicates clearly that it was not an immediate solution to the achievement problems of compensatory education. Some possible reasons for this are: (1) the contractors did not have effective programs; (2) one year is not enough time to make definitive judgment on the effectiveness of performance contracting in raising student achievements, especially in light of the developmental nature of all such programs; (3) the instrument used to measure what students learned may not have been sensitive to what students needed to learn and to what some contractors tried to teach; (4) students may not have fulfilled our expectation that they try as hard as they can to do as well as they can on the tests we administer to them.

Even though cognitive gains were disappointing, there are strong indications that performance contracting was effective in introducing new staffing patterns, new roles for teachers, students and parents, and new technology, into school systems traditionally resistant to innovation. A good measure of this is the way in which teachers themselves, at a number of former performance contracting sites, have shown interest and persistence in continuing the techniques, materials and activities originally introduced by the contractor.

It seems likely that performance contracting will continue on a limited scale for well-defined purposes. Some smaller, less-known companies will see performance guarantees as a good way to "break into the market." Some districts will see performance contracting as a good way to do research and development with new methodology and materials, while holding suppliers accountable for results. Vocational education is a promising area because of well-defined skill levels and performance norms. Finally, we may see much more of "internal" contracting in which the district contracts with teachers or teachers' associations for the achievement of specific performance objectives.

Edward B. Glassman
Office of Education
Department of Health,
Education, and Welfare

VIII

The concept of performance contracting appears to offer a way to effect an improvement in the management of education by:

- Acting as a change agent in the use of resources (teachers, equipment, materials, and time)
- Supporting changes in the organization of education (instruction, classroom, school, and district)
- Focusing attention on the need for better means of measuring program outcome and cost.

Performance contracts have permitted the local education agency to explore in a systematic manner alternative uses of equipment and materials. These instructional materials are not new to most districts; the *way* in which they are used is new. Additionally, the school has to make an explicit guarantee of its own—to insure a specified number of instructional hours. An hour of reading instruction becomes, in fact an *hour* of reading instruction for the student.

The greater individualization of instruction and the effective use of paraprofessionals has supported the feasibility of higher student-adult ratios as a way of changing the organization of the educational process. At the school and district level of organization, performance contracting has highlighted the benefit of a program focus in achieving an increased understanding of the resources required to produce specific outcomes. This may well hasten the demise of management by geographic location or grade-level and promote a management focus at the classroom level.

The most significant, and widely acknowledged, impact of performance contracting is the powerful impetus it has given to the efforts to develop better means of measuring program outcome and cost. This measurement improvement, almost alone, should have a far-reaching impact on the management of the resources of education.

Sue A. Haggart
Senior Staff Member
The Rand Corporation

IX

It is dangerous to pretend to draw conclusions now about performance contracting in education given our small store of experience. Nevertheless, two observations appear warranted. Performance contracting is not the holy grail of teaching; neither is it the handwriting on the wall signifying the end of the educationists' bureaucracy.

The promise it may hold for public education will not even be tested, much less fulfilled, unless experiments with the technique meet the following conditions:

1. The allocation of pre-experimental time and resources to achieve agreement among school district participants concerning the contract and its implementation.

2. Careful attention must be paid to mechanisms developed to facilitate the process of integration and internalization of innovation in the school.

3. Comprehensive evaluation using multi-dimensional

measures of performance contracting over time are needed. Additional measures of achievement, ones different from those traditionally used, are needed, as well as the examination of dimensions concerning other than academic learning, e.g., organizational climate, self-image, and sense of power.

4. Impacts such as contagion, stress, or rejection of the innovation by other units of organization also need to be understood.

5. Finally, evaluation designs should leave room for the discovery of unanticipated consequences.

For now, however, the studies on performance contracting tell us more about what is wrong with federal policy making than about the performance contracts. Federal policy choices influence the selection of goals and priorities by other educational authorities. So long as federal policy in education continues to search for the holy grail of instant results via narrowly defined efficiency measures, innovations are doomed to trivial outcomes. Until innovations are given a reasonable allocation of time for planning and start up, the innovation effort will be so much wasted resources. Our study of innovation and change will be characterized by ever learning and never coming to knowledge.

Laurence Iannaccone
Professor, Graduate School of
Administration and Graduate School
of Education, University of
California at Riverside

X

For approximately the first twelve months following the

introduction of guaranteed performance contracting in Texarkana, hundreds of school administrators jumped on the innovation bandwagon and still thousands of others talked about the eventuality of implementing a guaranteed performance contract in their school system. Now, the American public, particularly the educators, have become fully aware that guaranteed performance contracting is not the panacea that they thought it might have been. Allegations of teaching to the test and education being subsumed by the industrial complex have taken their toll. Most critical, however, is the fact that the guaranteed performance contract simply has not created the results in terms of educational achievement, that is, pupil output, that it initially was supposed to have done. What guaranteed performance contracting has done, however, is to create a mechanism for both accountability and management.

The ever-increasing demands of communities to be involved in educational decision-making have resulted in cries for school districts to make public their student achievement. Perhaps making education accountable for its output has been the major value of guaranteed performance contracting. I would contend, however, that most educators have been aware of output all along. They may not have owned up to their shortcomings, but they have always been very much aware of the difficulties they faced. The most significant value of guaranteed performance contracting, I believe, has been that in order to implement a guaranteed performance contract educators have had to take a long hard look at process. It is the changes to the process of education that will in the long run have the greatest impact on output.

Fewer than half of the number of companies engaged in performance contracts last year are similarly engaged during this school year. The future of guaranteed performance contracting can, therefore, be considered rather dim. However, the fact that guaranteed performance contracting is being phased out of the educational spotlight is not wholly bad. Performance contracting has served its purpose. It has succeeded in priming the pump of accountability, monitoring, and management and by doing so has created a group of educators more aware of process and output in that system which we call education.

Michael H. Kean
Assistant to the Superintendent
School District of Philadelphia

XI

My attitude toward performance contracting on the basis of the discussions at the joint AERA-AASA conference, and information and reflection, both prior to and subsequent to the conference, includes the following elements:

1. *Performance contracting and achievement improvement.* The weight of evidence to date seems to be that performance contract intervention does not consistently lead to better-than-average achievement gains. At best the verdict on performance contracting as a producer of better-than-average achievement has to be "not proven." Data thus far available do not permit any confident assertions with respect to amount of achievement gain per instructional dollar, but it seems altogether unlikely that the performance contract mode of instruction will loom as more efficient than conventional modes in this respect.

2. *Other presumed benefits of performance contracting.* Given the discouraging achievement gain outcomes associated with

performance contracts, there has been a disposition on the part of advocates of this mode of intervention to say that even in the absence of conspicuous improvements in achievement gains, performance contracting, nevertheless, had other significant values, e.g., increased flexibility, encouragement of open class-room approaches, innovative approaches, etc. These claims are worthy of attention, though it must be declared that the evidence in support of them is not highly persuasive; but even if one accepts these declarations, it is important to realize that the basis for discussion has been significantly altered: we are now asked to think of performance contracting as impacting process variables, not product, which is quite contrary to the bases on which performance contracting was originally most forcefully advocated.

3. *"Performance Contracting" as a variable.* Consideration of the results of the early performance contracting studies heightened the realization that "performance contracting" per se is a poor experimental variable. The variation from one performance con-tract experiment to another in effectiveness forces our attention to the quite variant modes of intervention that have been utilized in several performance contracting situations. It seems clear that it is simplistic to talk of the effect of "performance contracting" rather than to talk of the effects of the specific types of intervention that were the genuine experimental variables in the several projects. Methods, materials, and teacher competence, as well as degree of outside intervention, all varied from one project to another; it seems clear that the impact of these variables, separately and in combination, need be evaluated separately from the performance contracts' mode of intervention before any assertions can be made as to the special contributions or utility of the performance contract mode.

4. *Measurement aspects of performance contract activity.* Everyone recognizes that the measurement processes in the

conduct and assessment of performance contracted intervention leave much to be desired. There is special need for more rigorous attention to instrument selection in relation to the specific goals of the contract intervention, including most particularly metric properties of the instruments chosen in relation to considerations of reliability of growth measures; very much more careful planning of the measurement aspects of performance contract interventions with respect to such items as testing, training of examiners, security of instruments, etc.; far more advance attention to analysis of results in relation to performance contract goals; and far more advance attention to modes of collecting and reporting test information in relation to the terms of the contract. There is widespread feeling that most available standardized tests have significant limitations with respect to the fulfillment of measurement demands of performance contract situations, particularly when the duration of the performance contract intervention is limited—say, less than a year. Nevertheless, even with existing instruments it seems possible, at least in this observer's opinion, to do with careful planning a considerably improved measurement job in relation to performance contract programs than has typically been the case to date.

I think that the results of the OEO study and the attendant publicity may have, in fact, been the death knell of performance contracting. I would regard this as unfortunate, at least in the sense of implying a premature judgment of the efficacy of this mode of intervention. A full and fair evaluation of this arrangement for the provision of instructional support would require, in my judgment, a longer period, a more careful specification of outcomes, identification of ways of measuring outcomes and ways of relating performance contract outcomes to control of anticipated outcomes. I suspect that it is unlikely that performance contracts meeting these desiderata will be entered into in the foreseeable future. It became clear in the course of the AERA-AASA conference, if it had not been before, that the motivation prompting many school administrators to enter into performance contract arrangements had little to do with hoped for better-than-average increases in achievement—that administrators seized upon performance contract arrangements for other (though quite possibly no less worthy) purposes, which, in fact, may have been achieved, to some extent at least, through the performance contract interventions. An evaluation of performance contracting ought certainly recognize these perhaps hidden agenda, and suggest the utilities of performance contracting for the advancement of certain school management purposes, even in the absence of dramatic contributions to improved achievement.

> *Roger T. Lennon*
> *Senior Vice President*
> *Harcourt Brace Jovanovich, Inc.*

XII

My belief is that performance contracting may have value for American education. However, it has been so badly managed thus far that the idea is unlikely to receive the kind of thoughtful consideration it deserves, at least in the immediate future. It is especially unfortunate that performance contracting fiascos have discouraged interest in subcontracting, an idea which may have even greater relevance to our educational needs.

In my opinion, the opposition to performance contracting by teacher organizations was the natural and to be expected result of the ineptness of those who espoused and sought to implement the idea. While I regret that experience to date with performance contracts has been overgeneralized to mean that the concept has no utility for American education, I believe also that opposition to the performance contracts in existence or recently completed would have been greater if full information about their genesis and inadequate substantive rationale had been widely available.

Myron Lieberman
Director, Office of Program
Development and Administration
(Teacher Education)
City University of New York

XIII

Remember the principle of lighter-than-air vehicles, which was coupled with long-distance air travel in the form of the dirigible? Just about the time this innovation seemed promising, the tragedy of the Hindenberg disaster cut short the career of the dirigible. Yet, in other forms, we still have lighter-than-air as well as long-distance air travel. By analogy we are in the weeks after the Hindenberg crashed. It is impossible to predict what will happen, and somewhat difficult to characterize where we've been. Will we build more dirigibles? A different kind of aircraft? Crucify dirigible manufacturers? Abandon air travel? Has our experience anything much to tell us about what we might do next? I think some of the elements of performance contracting, as we've known it since 1969, will reappear in several guises. Vouchers is one such.

But whether OEO's blowing up of the Hindenberg will kill our dirigible, I just don't know.

James L. Mecklenburger
Phi Delta Kappa

XIV

   The full potential of performance contracting has not been realized and, in my opinion, warrants further careful study.

   Although a majority of research studies report negligible pupil achievement gains, many research experts emphasize the lack of appropriate, valid evaluation procedures and instruments for these studies. Evaluators and administrators involved in the programs appear to agree that performance contracting offers opportunities for low-risk, low-cost innovation and change.

   It seems to me that reports have minimized positive "by-product" values because they were not primary goals. For instance, some programs have resulted in decreased pupil dropout rates, but this fact has been overshadowed by emphasis on low gains in reading and math.

   I believe that performance contracting requires more time, with expertly devised evaluation, before valid judgments can be finalized. The resolution adopted by the AASA membership at their annual convention in February (1972) substantiates this position.

Resolution Adopted by the American Association of
School Administrators Annual Convention February, 1972

The pressures for change in public schools have never been greater. Taxpayers want more for fewer dollars, while school personnel bargain for increased wages. Governmental agencies and minority groups demand that minority-group children receive equal (not necessarily identical) educational opportunities; parents and community groups want to be involved in the planning and operations of schools; and pressures for accountability are multifaceted and real. Performance contracting has been suggested as one feasible solution to many of these problems.

We believe that performance contracting allows schools to experiment with and validate new learning systems with low risk and costs. We do not believe it has demonstrated total cost savings in overall school budgets, although it may do so in specific areas. We support the application of the concept by school districts with adequate evaluation so long as it is perceived as a means for effecting positive change.

Paul B. Salmon
Executive Secretary
American Association of
School Administrators

XV

My overall view of performance contracting is:
1. On the data presented at the Conference, the best contractor was doing very well, and the deviation from the mean

was significant enough to make it highly probable that we now have identified a procedure which can provide massive gains on basic skills, by contrast with the usual approaches.

2. On the data I have seen since, it appears extremely likely that several other contractors also produced substantial gains, a fact that was masked earlier by statistical and test artifacts.

3. Recent data on retention strongly suggests these gains are not transient; the Philadelphia tests by IDEA in fact suggest that retention is much better than with the usual procedures.

4. None of the data so far establishes long-term retention of substantial gains, and it is essential we follow up.

5. None of the data so far establishes cost-effectiveness advantages, but the main issue for many parents is effectiveness even at higher costs.

6. The reactions of most Conference participants suggested that they thought the appropriate standards for judging educational innovations are that big gains must be shown the first year by the median performer. You don't flunk the whole math class because the median student flunks. Education is in bad repute and bad condition not because successful procedures are unknown but because they are discarded as unfashionable rather than being developed and disseminated and quality-controlled.

7. One of the most important features of performance contracting is that it puts severe pressure on the contractor to look at the cost-effectiveness of the various procedures he might use. The educational scene has been badly lacking in agents on that reinforcement schedule until now. Of course, this will produce some abuses which we shall have to learn to control by improved contracts, auditing, and evaluation. But the present system performs so badly in teaching basic skills, by comparison with

schools in several other countries, that it is hard to avoid regarding
it as a far worse abuse.

Michael Scriven
Department of Philosophy
University of California
at Berkeley

XVI

The results of the Office of Economic Opportunity's Performance Contract Experiment indicate that participating private
firms operating under performance contracts in school year
1970-1971 did not perform significantly better than traditional
school systems. These findings are quite similar to those reported
by The Rand Corporation in its survey of non-experimental
performance contract programs.

OEO commented on its findings that "It is clear that there is
no evidence to support a massive move to utilize performance
contracting for remedial education. School districts should be
skeptical of extravagant claims for the concept."

This does not mean performance contracting is dead, but
does indicate the need for considerable development. Measurement techniques, incentive clauses, and contract administration
procedures need considerable refinement. The capabilities of
private firms themselves may also need development.

Performance contracting might best be considered as an
infant concept, that will change in the future. Varied applications
of it are possible including internal contracting by teachers,

incentive contracts for administrators or non-academic programs. The range of possible programs should not be underestimated. Nevertheless, such programs should be considered high-risk because of their undeveloped stage and pursued carefully.

Performance contracting has shown itself to be a simple concept, whose value was initially overestimated, that is complex in execution. Its long-range potential is presently unclear.

Charles B. Stalford
Office of Economic Opportunity

XVII

Performance contracting must still be considered in the realm of unproven innovations. It is innovative not because it is a new idea for groups to contract for and pay for services only after those services have been delivered in accordance with specifications, but because its application in education calls for payment to trainers only after learners have learned in accordance with learning specifications. This innovative application still must be considered unproven, since it is not at all clear that by following the practice of performance contracting students learn better than they otherwise would. Certainly before this innovative practice can be proven, it needs to be worked out technically better than it has so far. Thus, a variety of measurements and statistical problems must be solved before learning specifications associated with performance contracting can be adequately stated and tested. Before these technical problems are worked out, it would seem to me inadvisable for school districts to be overly zealous in entering into performance contracting with firms who are anxious to sell such services on other than a cost-sharing experimental basis.

Daniel L. Stufflebeam
Director, Evaluation Center
College of Education
Ohio State University

XVIII

The last chapter in performance contracting has not been written. New research is being conducted, the results of which refute many of the preliminary conclusions reported in the OEO experiment. These new findings lead one to question the conclusions reached in the OEO experiment, if not in fact the total project design, as well as the final treatment of data.

In the OEO experiment, preliminary conclusions were drawn by assuming all performance contracting companies had to be successful in all grades in order for performance contracting to be successful. This was not the design of the original project. No consideration was given in the final treatment of the data to reflect its impact on different age level students, different performance contracting programs or different student populations.

Several other independent studies have shown that though students in some of the experimental programs did not achieve one grade level gain in achievement, they more than doubled their output from previous years' experiences.

One such independent research project, conducted by Dr. Joan Webster* in the Grand Rapids Schools, refutes many of the OEO findings. Dr. Webster's research of a cost-effective model used two school age groupings—early elementary and junior high students—and included six reading programs; a control group using the systemwide adopted reading program; three different performance contracting companies' programs; a publisher's program; and a traditional remedial reading program.

Dr. Webster found no significant difference in reading achievement gain in any of the programs studied in the lower grades. However, she did find one performance contracting program significantly less costly than all the other programs. In the junior high programs, only the performance contracting companies' programs experienced a year's gain in reading achievement while the control group and the remedial reading groups achieved approximately one-third as much. The cost effectiveness of the programs again was significantly in favor of both performance contractors' programs; with one contractor's program being considerably less expensive than the other.

One might conclude from the results of this rather comprehensive study that there are significantly different cost-effective reading programs for underachieving children offered by some contractors. Further, the results would tend to indicate that performance contracting programs in reading may not be as adaptable and effective for early elementary children as for older children.

*Cost Effective Analysis of Six Reading Programs in the Grand Rapids Public Schools.

In view of the above, it is this writer's opinion that performance contracting still shows promise in raising the achievement level of some students but cannot be considered the one solution for all the learning problems in education.

Norman P. Weinheimer
Executive Director
Michigan School Boards Association

Appendix A
Participants and Staff

Mr. Charles L. Blaschke
President,
Education Turnkey Systems

Dr. George B. Brain
Dean, College of Education
Washington State University

Dr. Roald F. Campbell
Fawcett Professor of
Educational Administration
Ohio State University

Ms. Polly Carpenter
Senior Staff Member
The Rand Corporation

Dr. Richard A. Dershimer
Executive Secretary,
American Educational
Research Association

Ms. Donna Durgin
American Educational
Research Association

Dr. Robert L. Ebel
College of Education
Michigan State University

Dr. Stanley Elam
Editor
Phi Delta Kappan

Dr. William Ellena
Deputy Executive Secretary
American Association of
School Administrators

Ms. Martha Gable
Editor, *School Administrator*
American Association of
School Administrators

Dr. Robert Glaser
Learning Research and
Development Center
University of Pittsburgh

Dr. Edward B. Glassman
Department of Health,
Education, and Welfare

Ms. Sue A. Haggart
Senior Staff Member
The Rand Corporation

Dr. Laurence Iannaccone
Graduate School of
Administration and Graduate
School of Education,
University of California
at Riverside

Mr. Michael H. Kean
Assistant to the
Superintendent
School District of
Philadelphia

Dr. Roger T. Lennon
Senior Vice President
Harcourt Brace Jovanovich, Inc.

Dr. Donald M. Levine
(Conference Chairman)

Associate Professor
Teachers College
Columbia University

Dr. Myron Lieberman
Office of Program
Development and
Administration
(Teacher Education)
City University of New York

Mr. James L. Mecklenburger
Phi Delta Kappa

Dr. Paul A. Miller
U.S. Office of Education

Dr. Selma J. Mushkin
Public Services Laboratory
Georgetown University

Dr. William Russell
American Educational
Research Association

Dr. Paul B. Salmon
(Conference Co-Chairman)
Executive Secretary
American Association of
School Administrators

Dr. Michael Scriven
Department of Philosophy
University of California
at Berkeley

Dr. George N. Smith
Superintendent of Schools
Mesa, Arizona

Mr. Charles B. Stalford
Office of Economic Opportunity

The Honorable E.C. Stimbert
State Superintendent of
Public Instruction
State Department of
Education
Nashville, Tennessee

Dr. Daniel L. Stufflebeam
Evaluation Center
Ohio State University

Mr. Bro Uttal
Graduate School of Business
Harvard University

Dr. Norman P. Weinheimer
Michigan School Boards
Association

Appendix B

Advisors

Dr. Roald F. Campbell
Faculty of Educational
Administration
The Ohio State University

Dr. Jeanne Chall
Graduate School of Education
Harvard University

Dr. Robert L. Ebel
College of Education
Michigan State University

Dr. Edward B. Glassman
Department of Health,
Education, and Welfare

Ms. Sue A. Haggart
The Rand Corporation

Dr. Laurence Iannaccone
Graduate School of

Administration
University of California
at Riverside

Dr. Malcom Provus
University of Virginia

Dr. Robert Stake
School of Education
University of Illinois

Dr. Richard A. Dershimer
American Educational
Research Association

Dr. Terry Sarrio
American Educational
Research Association

Dr. William Ellena
American Association of
School Administrators

Appendix C
The Rand Research Strategy

The research strategy employed by Rand in the study reported on pages 35-48 of this volume combined several approaches: survey, case study, and quasi-experiment. Such a strategy is particularly adapted to real-life situations because it is flexible enough to accommodate unforeseeable changes, broad enough to make it unlikely that significant findings are over-looked, focused enough to pick up whatever experimental results may be derived, and general enough to assure that local quirks do not bias the findings.

The major objective of Rand's field monitoring and evaluation was to provide a realistic basis for the material to be incorporated in a *Performance Contracting Guide*. Particular emphasis was to be placed on uncovering features peculiar to performance contracting, as opposed to features to be found during the implementation of any new teaching approach. Programs appropriate for such a study were "native grown," that is, conceived and executed at the local level to answer local needs. These programs were too diverse for inter-program comparisons in any scientific sense. Thus, we decided at the outset to emphasize features of the environment in which the programs were carried out, such as planning and management, contract specification and settlement, teacher involvement, contractor participation, and

183

evaluation—as well as the instructional effectiveness of the programs.

A study this broad could take one of two tacks: either many programs could be reviewed in a relatively superficial manner, or a few programs could be studied in depth. To insure that conclusions were both valid and general, a mix of the two approaches was followed, with emphasis on the in-depth studies. The result was that 8 programs were studied in depth and 15 additional programs were reviewed to verify the generalizability of the conclusions.

First, the Rand team drew up a master list of information that would be needed. This included several hundred items concerning such matters as characteristics of the community and student populations, relationships between the school system and the community, teacher organizations, and school financial support. Particular attention was paid to the organization of the learning center, methods and materials used in instruction, training of program personnel, and provision of special incentives to students or teachers in the program. Similar information was gathered to describe regular classrooms or classrooms in other programs with comparable goals.

In general, a balanced plan of collection of quantitative data was attempted, and in every case interviews of key people were conducted, all relevant documentation was gathered, and—where necessary and possible—new data were generated.

A single researcher was given primary responsibility for organizing, conducting, and reporting on the work in each city. This provided continuity and insured that people involved with the program at the local level had ready access to the Rand team and vice versa.

The team members studying the programs in each city made several extended visits throughout the year. After a brief preliminary visit to establish contact with school personnel, a week or more was spent in observing the administration of pretests and the start-up phases of the program, and talking with administrators, teachers, contractors and other involved personnel. A more lengthy visit was made about midway through the program, during which extensive observations were made of program and regular classrooms, further interviewing was carried out, and additional data were gathered. Toward the end of the program another visit of a week or more was made to observe the posttesting and to obtain final reactions of key people to the program.

Polly Carpenter

DATE DUE

APR 18 75			
MAY 6 '88			
MAR 8 '90			
GAYLORD			PRINTED IN U.S.A.